MW01592419

There Goes My Heart

MARILYN COHEN SHAPIRO

This book is dedicated

to

Larry Shapiro

"Come my love and we shall wander just to see what we can find. If we only find each other still the journey is worth the time."

Janet Casey calligraphy print, 1980

ACKNOWLEDGEMENTS

Thank you to all my family and friends who told me their stories and gave me permission to share them with my readers.

Thank you to Laurie and Jim Clevenson of the Schenectady, New York's *The Jewish World* for publishing many of the stories in this book.

Thanks to the staff, faculty, and students at the Capital District Educational Opportunity Center for all you taught me in my years of working in adult education.

Thank you to Sol Writers for encouraging me to publish this book.

Thank you for the efforts of Mia Crews for bringing this project to life.

Thank you to my parents, Fran and Bill Cohen, who were always there for me.

Thank you to my children, Adam, Julie, and Sam, who give me so much joy.

And a special thank you to Larry Shapiro, my husband, my soulmate, my best friend, my muse, and the subject of (too!) many of my articles!

TABLE OF CONTENTS

INTRODUCTION

When I was fifteen years old, a friend and I attended a writer's institute at the State University of New York (SUNY) at Plattsburg. That week was to change my life. It only took me fifty years to see it through to fruition.

Chris was my closest friend. She was a year behind me in school, but we were soulmates. Chris was brilliant, insightful, and understood me. We spent innumerable hours listening to Simon and Garfunkel, taking walks near our homes in Keeseville, and talking about life and our future.

In the spring of 1966, we found out that SUNY Plattsburg was holding a one-week writer's workshop on its campus. The college was offering scholarships to local high school students. We both applied and both were accepted.

Our parents took turns driving the fifteen miles each day up to the campus. We took classes in fiction, non-fiction, and poetry. Chris gravitated towards poetry. I was more interested in personal essays and fiction, similar to what I had written for many years.

Since I could remember, I had kept a diary or journal. My first was a little blue book with a lock and key where I kept my innermost thoughts. I am sure my family, especially my brother, read it while I wasn't around. Our cat thought it was a great chew toy, as the ends were shredded with teeth marks. I doubt if I had many profound insights as a pre-teen. It must have been important to me, however, as I kept it tucked away in my night stand for decades. It finally got tossed when my husband Larry and I did "The Big Dump" in our 2015 move to Florida.

After the first diary was filled, I replaced it with a marbled composition book. Although my actual life in our small town was fairly tame, my narratives were filled will angst and passion. Directly across from my "No Trespassing!" warning on the inside cover, I wrote my first entry dated November 15, 1965. "Life can be cruel at times. It can be bitter, unhappy, and unstable. What you once enjoyed becomes boring; what you thought becomes childish and immature." Many of the entries dealt with my poor body image. "I weigh 127. I have to weigh 115! Breakfast: 1 egg, 1 toast 1/2 orange." ("Oh Marilyn," my adult self says. "Why were you so hard on yourself?")

A few pages later, the journal recorded one of my first crushes: "I met Jim on the white hills of Paleface Mountain when he was in my ski class." His face, which I thought would "always burn brightly in my memory," is a complete blur.

Along with the self-condemnations and the crushes were also attempts at short stories. Most of them revolved around adolescent self-discovery. A teen and her family deal with a sick grandparent. A young man finds the shadow of a mustache. A sensitive soul experiences hurt when a three-sided friendship becomes two-sided, and she becomes the outsider.

One of the longer works was a story about a girl who spends so much time on hair, make-up, and clothing for a dance she forgets the important things—like how to talk to a boy. "Maybe if I had worn the blue dress," says the first-person narrator as she gets ready for bed after she comes home, "someone would have asked me to dance."

This was the story I worked on during our week at the workshop. The day before it ended, I shared it with my instructor and the class. After I finished reading it aloud, there was silence followed by loud applause.

"Please meet our future writer," said my instructor. "She has a great deal of talent for a fifteen-year-old."

On the last day of the conference, all the attendees met on a beautiful green lawn on the campus. Awards were given to the adult attendees for best fiction, non-fiction, and poetry. I was given an award for best young writer.

Chris was thrilled for me, and she encouraged me to continue writing. That fall, I entered my junior year reassessing my future career goals. I had always wanted to be teacher, but this experience made me rethink that path and consider getting a degree in creative writing or journalism. My parents, however, strongly encouraged me to major in education. "Become an English teacher," my mother told me. "You can still be involved with writing, but you will have your summers off. And when you have children, you will be off when they are on vacation."

Feeling the pressure, I took the safer route and enrolled in the English education program at University at Albany. Chris was disappointed that I didn't pursue creative writing. Her graduation gift to me was a large blank journal with a black cover. "For your writing," she penned into the inside cover.

During my four years in college, I wrote innumerable essays for my coursework. For whatever reason, I never took one creative writing class the entire time. After I graduated, I taught high school for a short time. After I finished my masters in reading, I taught adult education classes, preparing people to take the exam for their GED or to have the reading, writing, and study skills needed for college. My favorite part was teaching how to write essays.

In the 1990s, I wrote a few articles for Schenectady, New York's *The Daily Gazette.* It wasn't until I retired that I started writing again. A chance meeting Jim and Laurie Clevenson, publisher and editor-in-chief respectively, of *The Jewish World* led to the opportunity to contribute personal essays to their bi-weekly newspaper.

To my delight, Chris and I recently reconnected. We shared

memories of the summer workshop, which for her provided a "long burning ember from the spark of the experience." She journals, composes haiku, and develops resources for social workers. Meanwhile, she is thrilled that I am finally following the path we started together fifty years ago this summer.

Barbara Kingsolver, award-winning novelist, poet, and essayist, stated, "There's no perfect time to write. There's only now." And *now* is perfect for me.

ONE

Camp: A Tale of Memory and Love

Growing up in Keeseville, New York, the only one I knew who went to sleep-away camp for most of the summer was a cousin in Long Island.

My siblings, friends, and I had enough to keep us busy in our small upstate town. From the first week of July through mid-August, the town offered arts and crafts at a building across from the high school. In the morning, buses shipped us off to swim lessons at Port Douglas, where we froze in Lake Champlain's chilly waters. Every afternoon, another bus would drive us again to Port Douglas beach for recreational swimming. On the days that I didn't feel like going to the beach, I was totally happy sitting on our side porch on an old chaise lounge reading The Bobbsey Twins, Nancy Drew, or The All-of-a-Kind Family. The only opportunities for my friends and me to go to a sleep-away camp were at church-run facilities or at Boy and Girl Scout locations. In 1961, four of us eleven-year-old girls from Keeseville spent one week at Camp Tapawingo at Point Au Roche on Lake Champlain, which was in operation as a Girl Scout camp in the 1960s. Julie, Margaret, Betsy and I were set up with several other campers in bunk beds housed in a lean-to. The structure had three walls and a roof, but the front area was wide open to the elements. "I remember the smell," recalled Betsy. "Woodsy and damp."

Meals were served in a large dining room. Each morning at breakfast, we were given a glass of orange or grapefruit juice, which we had to finish before we would get the milk to wash down the bitterness. Peanut butter and jelly on white bread was a staple for lunch. We swam, sang Girl Scout songs, told ghost stories, and ate s'mores around an open fire. We took a day hike. Everyone got sunburned and lined up for a coating of Noxzema that night. We did crafts, making long lanyards from plastic rope. We attempted archery and canoeing. We got bitten by mosquitos.

And we got homesick. Julie had to go to "Nursey" to have a cry, and I shed my own tears when I didn't get a letter from home. Why I expected mail when I was away for a week baffles me now, but at the time I felt deserted. But we had fun, despite the rain and the sunburns and the occasional tears.

Soon after our camping experience, Julie and her family moved twenty miles away, and Betsy and her family moved to Texas. Margaret and I stopped going to Girl Scouts, and we got involved in band and baseball and junior high angst.

Although I have lost touch with Margaret, I have kept in touch with Julie and Betsy all these years. Julie moved back to Keeseville in time to graduate with our class. Her in-laws had a cottage in Willsboro just down the road from my parents' place, and we would visit when she and her husband came down from Maine during the summer.

During my second pregnancy, I read M. M. Kaye's *Far Pavilions* and loved the main character Juli. I thought of my sweet friend from childhood. After some discussion, Larry and I chose the name Julie Rose, after my Grandpa Joe and Larry's Bubbe Rose. Julie and her husband moved to Austin, and we "see" each other on Facebook.

Betsy and I kept in touch with letters, holiday missives, and, more recently, Facebook. In 2014, I received an unexpected email from Betsy. She and her husband were coming to New York to see their son, who was a chef in New York City. They decided to take a side trip to

Glens Falls to see her grandmother's house. Would we like to meet them for dinner? Yes! I emailed back.

A few weeks later, Betsy came in my front door. We hugged each other, and almost fifty years apart melted away. "My best friend!" she whispered in my ear. We talked and talked, went out to eat together, and had a wonderful evening. We still keep in touch, and I promised her and Julie that I would stop by to see them in Texas on one of our future summer cross-country trips from Florida to Colorado.

When I was packing up the house for our move to Florida, I found on the bottom of an old trunk my green Girl Scout sash with the cloth merit badges along with group picture taken at Camp Tapawingo. Betsy is front row center; I am next to her, smiling a toothy grin; Julie is at the end. For a moment, I was eleven years old again, homesick, sunburned, and happy.

TWO

Some Enchanted Evening

I am a true believer in love at first sight. It happened to me on March 18, 1973.

The Jewish Singles group in Albany, New York, was having a Purim party at Herbie's Restaurant. A group of my girlfriends was going, and it seemed like a fun way to spend a Sunday evening. The notice recommended costumes, and I dragged along a long flowered dress I had purchased in New York City eight months before.

The event was taking place on the banquet room on the second floor of the restaurant. When I got to the top of the stairs, one of the organizers handed me a pink slip of paper. "It's for skits we're doing," he explained. "You're assigned to the pink group." I thanked him and scanned the room for my friends, who had arrived separately.

As I looked for them, I noticed a man standing across the room. I don't know what it was about him, but I immediately felt an attraction. Like the Rodgers and Hammerstein song from *South Pacific*, I felt as if that stranger across that crowded room was destined to be in my future. I noticed that he was holding a blue strip of paper.

When I located my friends, I saw that Debbie had a blue strip. "Debbie, change colors with me."

"Why?" she asked.

"I don't have time to explain," I said. "Just trade with me." She complied, and I changed into my "costume" and waited for instructions.

Steve, the party organizer, soon told us to find our groups by color and to plan a short skit with a Purim theme. The 'blue slip' group got together. We made quick introductions, and I formally met Larry Shapiro. The five of us decided to do a dating game, with the three women playing Queen Vashti, a gum snapping trollop, and Queen Esther. Larry was chosen to play King Ahasuerus, and the remaining member of our group played the host. The other groups also quickly arranged their skits, and each one performed. I had been taking pictures of the groups. Just before our group was "on," I asked Debbie to take a couple of pictures. The skit— as corny and as silly as the rest of the ones performed —went well. The king, played by Larry, chose the lovely Esther, played by me.

Forty years later, I am not sure if what followed was part chance, but I *am* sure that I had a hand in making sure of the outcome. After the last of the groups performed, Larry said, "Well, since I 'won' you in the Dating Game, would you like to share a hamantashen with me?"

That probably was one of the corniest pick-up lines in history, but it worked. Of course, by that point, I was willing to fall for anything he was going to offer. Over a prune hamantashen and some punch, Larry and I got to know a little about each other. He had never been to a Jewish singles event before. He and a friend were playing chess that afternoon and decided on a whim to head down from Saratoga Springs to Albany for the night. I learned about his background. He had gone to undergraduate college in Boston and had just completed his master's degree at Syracuse University. While looking for a job, he was working at his parents' store in Schuylerville and living with them in Saratoga Springs.

What impressed me was how much we had in common. Both of us had grown up in fairly small towns and belonged to small synagogues. Both of our parents operated small, family run department stores in upstate New York. Both of us were one of four children, with the same birth order: a girl, a boy, a girl (coincidentally both named Marilyn), and an unexpected girl a few years later. The more we talked, the more I was smitten with his warm smile, his intelligence, and his pleasant demeanor. My first impression was correct: I knew I wanted to see him again. However, he didn't seem to be getting any closer to asking for my phone number. My devious mind started working again. I had noticed that there was a sign-up sheet for a Jewish Singles event at the beginning of May. Although I knew that I would be visiting my parents in upstate New York that weekend, I put down my contact information in bold letters. Hopefully, he would take the bait.

As the evening drew to a close, Larry and I said our goodbyes, and I reconnected with my friends. Debbie gave me back my camera, and I was surprised to see that she had taken ten pictures of our Dating Game skit. "Why did you take so many?" I asked. "I don't know. I just kept snapping away," she explained.

The next night, I called my mother. "Last night I met the man I am going to marry," I announced.

I filled her in on the Purim party. She asked, "Did this man ask you out?"

"Not yet," I said.

"So he asked for your number?"

"No, not exactly," I said. "But I put it on a sign-up sheet for another event, and he will call."

My mother was not as confident as I was. But, sure enough, the next night, Larry called to ask me out to a movie for the following weekend. The sign-up ruse had worked! We saw *Man of La Mancha* at the movies, and then we went to Friendly's restaurant for a chocolate Fribble for Larry and a hot fudge sundae with vanilla ice cream for me.

The rest, as it is said, was history. We dated over the next few months, Larry proposed to me on our walk home from Rosh Hashanah services on September 28, and we announced it to our families after Yom Kippur was over on October 6. The road to the wedding was not as smooth as the first six months of our relationship, but that is another story.

And those pictures Debbie had snapped? When I developed the Kodak roll a month later, I realized she had captured the hour Larry and I first met. In my favorite, I am sitting in a chair with the other potential wives of Ahasuerus. I am looking up at my future husband with stars in my eyes.

In this day of dating websites, social networking, and speed dating, it is a little embarrassing to relate our own meet-up. Larry's reaction is always the same. "You're not telling that story again! It's too dorky!"

He's right. But I know that dorky meeting, with its blue slips of paper, the long flowered dress (which I kept in my closet for thirty-six years), and prune hamantashen was *b'shert*, meant to be. And as Larry and I work our way through our fifth decade of marriage, that tale of that enchanted evening will always be one of *my* favorite love stories.

THREE

Teaching Kids: A Great Idea?

I realized early in my adult life that there is a big difference between the career I envisioned in a classroom and the job I actually had.

I dreamed of being a teacher since I was a child. By the time I was six, I would set my dolls—and my sister Bobbie when she was old enough—around my stand-up chalk board and teach them the alphabet. By the time I was in high school, I had determined that I would go to college for a teaching degree. My love of reading, my interest in creative writing, and some pressure from my parents to choose a practical major made English education the right choice. Every spring, Keeseville Central held Student Teacher's Day. Those of us who were interested and considered responsible were allowed to take over the classes of the teachers. In both my junior and senior years, I had the opportunity to 'student teach' for two of my English teachers. I spent hours preparing lessons on Greek and Roman mythology, *The Outsiders* by S. J. Hinton, and vocabulary. I loved my role as "teacher for a day," and it confirmed my career path.

For my first two years at University at Albany, I completed required coursework through the English department, along with necessary classes in science, French, history, and music. By my junior year, I was taking education courses that prepared me for teaching. In my English methods class, I put together a multi-week unit plan on the theme of War and Youth. My project not only received top grades but also was used as a model for several years in the English education department. In my senior year, I finally had a chance to student teach at Mont Pleasant High School. I thrived in front of the classes. I loved putting together the lesson plans, the quizzes, the tests. I spent hours planning and producing the necessary paperwork, but it was worth every minute to implement it. I was rewarded in the end with a five plus out of five score. My supervisor wrote in his evaluation that I was a 'born teacher' who was a 'natural in front of the classroom.'

As the graduation date grew near, I started applying for a teaching position. It was a tough time to get a job as there were not many openings. Despite my excellent evaluation and decent grades, I couldn't even get an interview. In late June, however, a month after graduation, a break came through. A high school English teacher in a small town near Albany, New York, had handed in his resignation the last day of school as he had decided to enroll in a master's program. The principal wanted to fill the position before he left for his summer vacation. I interviewed for the job and was hired on the spot.

There was only one difficulty: the teacher I was replacing taught unusual classes. Along with a standard tenth grade English class, he taught numerous electives on creative topics including supernatural fiction, science fiction, the police state in literature, and the American cinema. The books had been ordered, the students had already signed up their courses before they left for the summer, but he had left no specific lesson plans. Over that summer, I read the novels and began developing the curriculums as best as I could.

The tenth grade students I greeted that first day took the change in teachers in stride. The juniors and seniors who had signed up for the electives, however, were disappointed to find that the teacher they expected was gone. Instead they had a new, young teacher with high ideals and higher expectations.

This challenge was even made more difficult by what I learned from the students. My predecessor had held séances during the supernatural classes, and the students in cinema had spent time making movies. I was at a complete loss in the police state course. The books ordered for the class included *Brave New World* and *1984.* Unfortunately some of the students were reading two or three years below grade level, certainly way below the level of the novels attached to the course.

The result was an absolute disaster. Despite a supportive principal and supportive faculty, I was in over my head. I spent every minute out of class, including weekends, working on lesson plans, projects, and quizzes. Unfortunately, the techniques that had served me so well in methods classes and student teaching fell flat. In addition to my difficulty with the implementation, I also was challenged by maintaining discipline. I was twenty-two years old, highly idealistic, and totally out of tune with students who lacked motivation and any interest in what I was trying to do. Although the majority of the students were well-behaved, a small group made it a point to see if they could disrupt my class. They talked, they threw spitballs, they refused to participate. It was a horrible experience. After spending years dreaming about being a teacher, I realized that nothing I had done in college had ever prepared me to handle a real class, a real job.

By June, I was exhausted, stressed, and seriously wondering if I could learn enough from my first year to handle a second year in the classroom. But the worst moment of that first year was yet to come. About three weeks before graduation, yearbooks came in. Students were passing around their own copies for signatures from classmates and from teachers. Two seniors, the children of highly respected members of the community, approached me with big smiles, asking me to sign their yearbooks. When they handed them to me, I was shocked and stunned to see that they had both drawn swastikas around my picture. I slammed the offensive books shut, refusing to sign and making some comment about how someday they would look back on their yearbooks with shame. I told the principal, who called them in. I don't remember the outcome of that discussion.

I did return in September. I was more confident, more organized, more prepared. However, I found teaching high school an uphill battle, a completely different experience than what I had dreamed. I left in January, eighteen months after I started and enrolled in the master's program in reading at University at Albany. I subsequently got a job teaching adult education at the Capital District Educational Opportunity Center, a division of Hudson Valley Community College. It was in that scenario that I found my niche. Classes were small and individualized, and I found it easy to relate to adult students. Many of them were highly motivated and focused in their wish to improve their reading and writing skills and obtain their General Equivalency Diploma (GED).

Now, many years later, I still look back on my first teaching job. I wonder if I could have done more to find a way to hold on until I gained enough experience and maturity to handle the real high school classroom. I also wonder what happened to those two students who got so much pleasure that day from seeing my face when I saw those hated Nazi symbols next to my picture. Did they forget about it as soon as they graduated? Did their yearbooks end up on a dusty shelf, never to be looked at again? Do they occasionally pull them out like I have done with my own high school yearbook and reminisce over pictures of their friends and their extra-curricular activities? Or do they come across my picture and feel regret, embarrassment and shame?

FOUR

Popping the Question: Can One Count the Ways?

Valentine's Day! On this most romantic holiday, there will be many marriage proposals. Some will be simple and old-fashioned: After getting the father's blessing, a nervous man will bring his girlfriend to a quiet intimate spot, go on bent knee, and pop the question. For others it will be a huge production that involves elaborate planning, intrigue, and at times a huge cast of characters to carry it off. Thanks to social media, this intimate moment has recently evolved into a very public "how-many-hits-can-my-proposal-get-on-You Tube?" event. No matter how couples get engaged, each story is unique, memorable, and forever part of their love story.

Larry intended to ask me to marry him on a grassy knoll at the Saratoga National Battlefield. Unfortunately, seconds before he was about to pop the question, he was stung by a bee. His lip began to swell, and we left hastily to find an ice pack. Two weeks later, we were walking home from Rosh Hashanah services in Saratoga Springs. Larry started talking about where we would live and how many children he would like us to have. When I asked him if this was a proposal, he quickly said, "No!" A few minutes later, as we were putting our coats away in a bedroom at his parents' home, he asked, "So you want to get married?" I said yes, we started to kiss, and Corky, the Shapiros' dog, jumped up and licked my face. Very romantic. We didn't even share the news with the family until eight days later at the Yom Kippur break-the-fast.

Thirty-five years earlier, my parents' engagement came after a whirlwind romance. After they had been maintaining a long-distant relationship for less than six months, my father came down to New York City from Alburgh, Vermont, to see my mother for the weekend. They had just seen *Gone with the Wind,* and my father proposed while they were having dessert in a coffee shop. "We were blinded by the movie," my mother recalled sixty-five years later. "He thought I was Scarlett O'Hara, and I thought he was Rhett Butler. Of course I said yes."

My brother needed more time and certainly more of a push. Jay had been dating Leslie for over a year when they stayed with my parents at their cottage on Willsboro Point on Labor Day weekend. On Sunday night, Jay suggested to Leslie that they take a walk to the rocky promontory overlooking Lake Champlain. The sun was setting, the crickets were chirping, and Burlington lights twinkled in the distance—Leslie was sure this was "The Moment." Nope. Jay just walked her back to the cottage. The next day, on the car ride back to Ithaca College, Leslie pressed for a commitment. "Give me one good reason why we should not get engaged," Leslie recalled. When Jay failed to come up with any, Leslie announced, "Fine! We're engaged!" It certainly wasn't the romantic proposal that Leslie was dreaming of, but forty-five years later their commitment and marriage are going strong.

Leslie wasn't the only one to reverse the roles in the proposal process. After graduating from Oberlin, Judy and Charlie were living together, unusual and not universally acceptable in 1971. Judy got tired of lying to everyone at work about her "roommates" and dealing with her parents' unhappiness with the situation. "I asked Charlie, 'Do you want to get married?'" Judy recalled. "He said 'Sure. Why not?'" They tied the knot six weeks later.

Debbie and Jim, both who had previously been married, had been dating for about a year, Debbie finally said to Jim, "So are we getting married or what?" They said their 'I do's' in Jamaica that summer.

After dating for several months, Diane and Mark were discussing with a group of friends at their weekly bowling night the topic of keeping a kosher home. Mark, the son of a kosher butcher, stated that he wouldn't marry anyone who didn't follow the Jewish dietary laws. Diane burst into tears, stated that she had no intention of doing so, and headed to the ladies' room for a good cry—and a change of heart. "When I returned," said Diane, "I cuddled up to him and told him I'd keep kosher." That promise sealed the deal. They were married a few months later and have lived *kashruthly* ever after.

Another couple's engagement came after the evening from hell. On a freezing cold December night in Baltimore, Becky and Mark had made plans to go to a concert followed by dinner at the Playboy Club. While trying to find the concert venue, they got hopelessly lost in a questionable section of town.

The situation deteriorated dramatically when Mark's old car, "The Purple Monster," sputtered and stopped dead. They both got out of the car, Mark lifted the hood, and the engine burst into flames. Mark yelled to Becky, "Quick! Give me your coat!" Becky quickly ripped it off, handed it to him, and watched in horror as Mark used it to smother the fire.

Mark walked to a pay phone to contact AAA, leaving Becky alone, nervous, and shivering in the car with her smoke-smelling coat. They never made it to the concert or out to dinner. When they finally got back to his apartment, they were tired, cold and hungry.

"Any girl that is willing to go through all of that with me and still come home cheerful is the girl I want to spend my life with," Mark said. "Will you marry me?" By that time, Becky had warmed up enough to say a resounding "Yes!"

For Becca, it was a rainy November night in Buenos Aires when she knew she would spend the rest of her life with Rolando. Becca tells it best:

"Ever so gently he kissed me-as softly as the rain falling into the dark night. 'We will be married,' he said, his dark eyes looking deeply into mine," recalled Becca. "It was not a question. It was not a proposal. It was simply and forever understood that we belonged together—no matter the distance. No matter the obstacles. And, to this day, the sound of raindrops softly falling reminds me of the promise of our eternal love."

Wow, Becca! Your story sure beats everything I have seen on You Tube. Happy Valentine's Day to you, Rolando, and all the couples celebrating their love.

FIVE

Let Them Eat Cake, But Understand the Commitment

In a *Dennis the Menace* cartoon published in 1973, just before Larry and I got engaged, the eponymous five-year-old and his friend Joey are looking into a bakery window at a multi-tiered, highly decorated wedding cake. Joey looks mesmerized, but Dennis is not impressed. "After the cake is gone," he says, "you'd still be married."

In my lifetime, I have seen many wedding cakes at many weddings. I have realized that the most important part of getting married is not the size of the cake or the grandeur of the festivities but the quality of the relationship and the depth of the love in the months and the years that follow.

My parents' wedding in 1940 was certainly not elegant. It was held in New York City on a Tuesday night in a hall whose costs were offset by the twenty-five cents given to the hatcheck girl. My father and mother made a handsome couple under the *chuppah*, Bill in his rented tuxedo ($7) and Fran in her rented wedding gown and floor length veil ($18). After the ceremony, guests were served tea sandwiches, fruit, and wedding cake. Unfortunately, by the time the photographer finished taking pictures of the happy couple, many of the guests had left. Nevertheless, their marriage lasted 68 years. (Priceless!)

Larry and I were married at Congregation Agudat Achim in Schenectady, New York, on a sunny, warm September afternoon in 1974. The ceremony was a little long. Larry admitted to me many years later that if the rabbi had talked any more, he, the impatient and hungry groom, would have left the *bima* early and headed for the hors d'oeuvres. The meal contained peas, even though we had specifically asked them to NOT include them on the menu (Larry hated peas!). The band completely botched the words to our first dance, Barbra Streisand's *He Touched Me*. The wine my parents had purchased up north in Plattsburgh was not kosher and almost wasn't served. My mother told the caterer, "I don't care! Just cover the darn bottles with tin foil and pour it!" During the course of the afternoon, my father, a little tipsy on the almost rejected wine, took to the microphone to thank Keeseville National Bank for financing the event. To top it all off, Larry spent most of our honeymoon in a Quebec City hospital dealing with a kidney stone. Despite our less-than-perfect nuptials, our marriage has flourished for over four decades.

The majority of the weddings Larry and I have attended have followed a similar pattern: white bridal gowns, rented tuxedos, synagogue or church settings, large receptions with multiple course meals, a band or a DJ, and lots of wine and dancing. Each one has been unique, but not a one any more special than the less conventional ceremonies we've attended.

My niece Laura and her husband Paul had their wedding on a beautiful summer's day in the gardens behind the Arlington, Massachusetts, library. Less than twenty-five people were in attendance, with Laura's Uncle Max officiating. After Paul crushed the wine glass, the newlyweds turned on a battery operated CD player and danced to Alison Krause's *When You Say Nothing At All*. Then everyone convened to a seafood restaurant for the wedding reception. Laura and Paul now have two beautiful children and an adorable Australian Labradoodle puppy named Cooper. Laura once posted on Facebook that Paul had suggested that they create more "just us" time by going out onto their yard and picking up the dog's poop together. Laura posted, "Thirteen years of marriage, and Paul is still a romantic!"

When my daughter Julie got engaged to Sam in 2006, Larry and I were thrilled and more than happy to start off their married life with a traditional wedding in a large hall with many relatives and friends in attendance. After several months of researching numerous options, Julie and Sam opted for a destination wedding at a resort near Moab, Utah. Just the immediate family was invited: Larry and I, our son Adam and a girlfriend, Sam's parents, and Sam's two sisters. The day before the wedding, all ten of us went to Arches National Park and hiked up to Delicate Arch, where we posed for a group photo. Julie and Sam were married on a brilliant May afternoon on the banks of the Colorado River with the rock formations from Arches as the backdrop. After dinner in the resort's restaurant, we shared a flourless chocolate cake topped with the two figures from our own wedding cake thirty-three years earlier. The next morning, several of us took a white water rafting trip down the Colorado River. All of us treasure the memories of that long weekend in Utah where we celebrated not only the love between two special people but also the beauty and wonder of an iconic national park and the twisting, historic river that runs near it.

A marriage doesn't have to last decades to be successful. We have a number of friends whose first marriage, for whatever reason, didn't work, but their second marriage is going strong. Most of their second weddings were small affairs. And we also have friends and relatives who have never legally tied the knot but are involved in successful long-term relationships. In all these cases, the wedding didn't make the marriage. Their commitment to each other did.

Barbara de Angelis, author and relationship consultant, wrote, "The real act of marriage takes place in the heart, not in the ballroom or church or synagogue…not just on your wedding day, but over and over again." Exactly, Barbara! No matter how big or how small the wedding, it is what endures through the years that follow that is important.

SIX

A Wedding Tale Filled With Love and Pain: This Too Shall Pass

Larry and I were married on a beautiful September day in 1974. The memories of our wedding day are somewhat hazy, captured in the beautiful wedding album that sits on our bookshelf. However, our honeymoon is one of the most memorable…and unusual…on record.

Our first night as man and wife, we stayed in a hotel in Glens Falls, New York. The next morning, we headed up to Quebec City for what we planned to be a romantic week in one of the oldest cities in North America.

Larry had made the arrangements to stay in a hotel that had opened just weeks before. Our room was large and spotless with a huge king-sized bed and a beautiful view of the city. Once we finished checking it out, we went out to dinner at a restaurant in the Old City, a charming old building with stone walls and a fireplace. We both enjoyed French onion soup and steak and returned to our hotel room.

At two o'clock in the morning, Larry woke up in agony with severe pains and cramps in his lower back. He thought he had food poisoning, maybe the French onion soup? He tried walking around the room, but in the end he just curled up in a ball on our king sized bed and moaned. After an hour of no relief, we realized we needed medical help.

The hotel was so new that the phone in our room didn't work. So I threw on some clothes and went down to the front desk to ask for a doctor. He showed up at four o'clock and quickly diagnosed Larry's pain as a kidney stone. The doctor gave Larry a shot of morphine. He gave *me* the name and address of the closest hospital with instructions to take him there first thing the next morning. Larry fell into a drugged sleep, and I watched him from the couch. Kidney stones? I knew nothing about kidney stones. I figured that he would be on dialysis the rest of his life. I stayed up the entire night trying to envision life taking care of an invalid.

Early the next morning, I packed up our bags, checked out of our beautiful hotel, and drove Larry to the local hospital's emergency room. His X-ray confirmed that he, indeed, had a kidney stone, a hard, crystalline mineral material formed within the kidney or urinary tract. While kidney stones are painful—described by sufferers even worse than the pain of childbirth or broken bones— we were assured that they are not life threatening. No, he would not be on dialysis for the rest of his life. However, since he was in a great deal of pain and far away from home, the doctor recommended that Larry stay until he either (1) passed the stone; or (2) had surgery to remove it. So Larry checked into his $400 a night hospital room. Once I knew he was comfortable, I checked into a nine dollar a night boarding house across the street that was recommended by the hospital staff.

Outside of our doctor, everyone else in the hospital and boarding house spoke French. I had taken the language for five years in high school and a semester in college. Surprising even myself, I was soon able to carry on limited conversations with the nurses, the patients, and their families. By the end of the week, we were engaging in long chats in French, punctuated by broken French—*moi!*—and broken English— the native *Québécois*.

My poor husband, however, didn't remember any of his two years of high school French. I walked over from the boarding house each morning, and we spent the day together—when I wasn't chatting with "*mes nouveaux amis*"—holding hands and watching French television. To add insult to injury, his roommate's doctor's prescription to pass the stone was for him to drink beer—lots of it. So every night, a group of his family and friends came over with several six packs of Molson's, and they had a grand old time. Unfortunately, the beer didn't flush out the stone. Larry's roommate had surgery on Wednesday to remove it.

The same fate was to befall Larry on Thursday. The surgery was considered 'minor,' but it required 'retrieving' the stone. Ouch! Not a great way to start off married life.

On Friday, Larry, now stone-free, was released from his "honeymoon suite." We began our trip back to New York. We thought it best that Larry didn't drive, so I took the wheel. While Larry dozed, I zipped down the highway, merrily keeping pace with the numerous trucks heading for the border. At one point, Larry woke up, looked at the speedometer, and yelled out, "You're going ninety miles an hour!" Whoops. Larry had me pull over, and he cautiously drove the rest of the way.

As originally planned, Larry and I stopped over at my parents' cottage on Lake Champlain on the way to Albany, but two days earlier than expected. My mother took one look at our sad faces and immediately assumed the marriage had already tanked. We quickly explained where we had spent the last five days. Our marriage was still intact, although our honeymoon was definitely a disaster.

Larry and I tried to make up for our lost honeymoon several times before getting it right. The next summer we headed to Nantucket, only to be delayed for a couple of days by a hurricane. The next trip was to Washington, DC, where gale winds closed down the National Zoo and knocked out all the electricity in our expensive hotel. We certainly got past all those vacation missteps, as we are celebrating over forty years of marriage. Yes, our marriage is written in stone, partly in kidney but mostly in love.

SEVEN

My Two Moms: How I Got Married and Gained an Extra Set of Parents

Larry has a special connection to Mother's Day: He was born on this Hallmark Card Holiday on May 9, 1948.

I can only imagine the joy Doris and Ernie felt when their second child, a son, was born. He was a beautiful baby. From what I heard from his mother and older sister, Larry was an easy child. He was quiet, never got into trouble, and spent most of his time either in his room or with his friends on the baseball field. He grew up, went to college at Northeastern University, and completed his master's degree at Syracuse University.

By the time he finished graduate school, Larry's parents were more than anxious for him to meet a nice Jewish girl and settle down. After meeting me at the Purim party, Larry kept me under wraps until the end of May, when he invited me to his house. I had a major strike against me; I had completely forgotten his birthday, which fell on Mother's Day that year. But Doris let that pass once Larry brought me home. Jewish? Check! Nice family? Check! Single and available? Double check! By the end of June, she and Larry's Bubbe Rose, began to put some pressure on Larry. So what if we had only been dating for three months?

"So what is your relationship with this person?" Doris asked.

"I guess we're going steady," Larry replied.

"Steady, shmeady," huffed Bubbe Rose. "She's a nice Jewish girl. You don't go steady. You get married."

Larry and I dated through the summer. By August, we were already talking marriage. Of course, we didn't share that with our families, but Doris was still working on it. One day, she showed me her engagement ring. "Whoever marries my son will wear this ring," she told me. Very subtle!

When his first attempt at proposing to me in Saratoga National Battlefield was thwarted by a bee sting, Larry tossed romance out the window and asked me to marry him after Rosh Hashanah services on September 28. We shared the news with my parents over the phone, but we saved our big announcement for his parents at the Yom Kippur Break-the-Fast on October 6, which coincided with Ernie's birthday.

"I have a special birthday present for you, Dad," Larry announced over coffee and birthday cake.

"Another ugly tie?" snorted one of his sisters.

"No, I'm giving you a daughter-in-law."

Everyone started hugging us and yelling "*Mazel tov*!" Doris was true to her summer promise. She ran into the bedroom, grabbed the engagement ring, and put it on my finger. I am sure I am one of the only people in the world who had her future mother-in-law place an engagement ring on her finger. Again, very subtle!

After that day, Mr. and Mrs. Shapiro became "Mom and Dad." I was really fortunate in that I now had two sets of parents who loved me deeply. Larry's parents treated me as well as, if not sometimes better, than they treated their own children. Mom, happy with Larry's choice, often kiddingly said, "If you two ever get divorced, I get custody of you." I may not have been able to make a brisket or a bed as well as my mother-in-law, but for the most part, I could do no wrong. When we delivered two grandchildren, it was the icing on the cake.

Throughout their lives, Mom and Dad were wonderful in-laws. They took great joy not only in their children's accomplishments, but also in the accomplishments of their daughter/sons-in-law. They adored their seven grandchildren and showered all of us with their love and their generosity for many years.

My parents and Larry's parents hit it off from the first time they met. Over the years, they spent many happy times together as dear friends as well as *mishpocha*. When they both retired, my in-laws purchased a condo a minute's walk from my parents. Ernie and Bill golfed; Doris and Fran shopped and shared confidences over coffee.

When Larry's mother died during heart surgery in April 1994, we were all devastated. And when Larry's father followed her a mere eight months later, the grief was overwhelming. Since their passing, so many wonderful events have occurred where they were not there physically but were there in our hearts. At so many occasions—bar and bat mitzvahs, graduations, weddings, the birth of their great-grandchildren—at least one of the children or grandchildren have said, "Mom and Dad would have been so proud!"

One Chanukah, I gave Larry's mother a framed poem entitled "My Other Mother" The first lines read, "You are the mother I received/the day I wed your son/And I want to say/Thank you Mom for the loving things you've done." She kept it on the wall in her bedroom. After she died, I took the poem and hung it in our bedroom, next to our wedding picture. So on this Mother's Day, I want to tip my hat to my two moms, the one I received at birth and the one I was given through marriage.

EIGHT

There Goes My Heart

The first week of September in Upstate New York is a time for new clothes, sharpened pencils, and bright yellow buses that reappear on neighborhood streets like clockwork two days after Labor Day. School opening is an important time for the children. It is also a bittersweet moment for the adults who are saying good-bye to them.

My first vivid memory was *my* first day of school. My mother walked me up the hill to the big brick building that housed all the grades for Keeseville Central. I quietly sat at a table stringing colored beads in Mrs. Ford's kindergarten classroom. My mother wordlessly slipped out the door. I didn't cry.

I was supposed to be the last of my parents' three children going off to school, but that plan failed. My sister was born three months before I entered kindergarten. Bobbie was a shining example of the little "surprise" many pre-birth-control women in their mid to late thirties experienced just when they thought diapers and formula were behind them. I am not sure if my mother pushed Bobbie in the carriage into the classroom that morning. I *am* sure dropping me off only to return to a house still equipped with a crib, a high chair, and a playpen was an ironic moment in my mother's life.

When it came time to send my son Adam off to kindergarten, I had mixed feelings. I was happy for him to be starting on his next adventure, but my mind was filled with concerns. Would his teacher, who had a reputation for being strict, be kind to my son? Would he overcome his shyness, make new friends? My fears were certainly not alleviated when within the first week he didn't come up our driveway after the school bus pulled away. My phone call to the school triggered an alert to the driver, who found Adam fast asleep in the back the bus. Somehow, he *did* survive his first year. Life before school became a distant memory as Julie followed Adam up the school bus steps three years later.

What was so much more difficult for me was sending Adam off to college. The summer before, I shopped for comforters and dorm sized sheets and enough shampoo and soap to last him four years. The thought of his leaving the house and our no longer having four at the dinner table caused me to tear up all summer. A week before he was to leave, I was cutting up several pounds of chicken breast when I burst into tears. "I will never have to make this much chicken again!" I sobbed out loud to an empty kitchen.

The night before we drove him to the University of Rochester, most of the purchases were still in bags with the tags still on them. Unlike me who needed to be packed and ready days in advance, Adam was happy to just stuff things into suitcases and plastic bins at the last minute.

The four of us lugged his life in Rubbermaid containers up the five flights of stairs—why did my children always get the top floors of their dorms?—and Adam quickly settled in. My last memory of my son that day was his leaning back on his chair in front of his desk, proclaiming "I am going to like it here!"

Once Larry, Julie, and I got back into the car for our trip home, I felt such deep pain that I thought someone had wrenched my heart out of my body. I cried from Rochester to Syracuse. I finally stopped when Julie commented sarcastically from her perch in the back seat, "You have another child, you know!"

Sending Julie off to Williams College three years later was a little easier—maybe because she was the second child; maybe because she was only forty-five minutes away. We dropped her off in Williamstown, Massachusetts, and got her situated in her fourth floor—of course!—dorm room. By the time we pulled into our driveway, we were giddy with excitement over our new-found freedom. We knew that both children were happy in their college environment. That knowledge, coupled with the realization that we no longer had to worry about the daily angst of their high school lives— homework, car pools, dates for a dance—made the transition into our now empty nest smoother.

Still, each time our children came home, I found their inevitable departure difficult. After sending Julie off to college for her final year, I asked my mother if she ever got used to saying goodbye. "Oh, Marilyn," she said. "It never gets easier! Every time any one of you gets into the car and drives away, I think to myself, 'There goes my heart!'"

So, each year on the first day of school, when I see the school bus filled with children with their new clothes, their sharpened pencils their bright back packs, I will be thinking of my first day, my children's first days, and my aching heart.

.

NINE

Where Have You Gone, Leslie Bush?

Like many other boys who grew up during the 1950s and early 1960s, my husband Larry collected baseball cards. Each spring and summer, Larry would walk, run or bike to the corner market near his home in Saratoga Springs, New York, where he would exchange his nickel for a new hot-off-the-presses pack of cards. Once he entered high school, Larry lost interest and never again got caught up in the rush of completing a major league season's set. There was only one exception, a caramel-coated summer when Larry took our family on a sweet journey to complete a set of cards highlighting baseball players from almost eight decades before.

Through the classic song, "Take Me Out to the Ballgame," baseball has always been linked with a popular popcorn and peanut confection that included a prize in each red, silver, and blue box. In the summer of 1993, one of the snacks' promotions was a series of reproductions of two dozen 1915 baseball cards. Larry decided to buy a three-pack combo in order to see what the cards looked like.

Of course, like the saying associated with a famous potato chip, Larry just couldn't stop at just one. After obtaining his first three cards, replicas of Christy Mathewson, Napoleon Lajoie, and Walter "Rabbit" Maranville, he was hooked—and determined to collect all twenty-four cards. Every time he went shopping, he brought home three to six more boxes to see which cards he could add to his pile.

Our children, Adam and Julie, more than happy to eat the sweet treat, soon joined their father in his quest. Forty-five boxes later, along with thirty duplicates, we were up to fifteen of the two dozen cards. As we all became more determined, we bought and ate more boxes. We learned that the hot summer weather would make the contents of open boxes sticky and soft, and the solution was to keep them in the refrigerator. The sugar coated treat became the snack of choice and the number one offering to anyone who came to visit.

As the weeks progressed, and the refrigerator became more filled with half-eaten, somewhat stale boxes, the quest became even more difficult. Seventy-two boxes later, we had collected twenty-one cards, as well as doubles, triples, and even quadruples of baseball immortals such as Ed Walsh of the Chicago Americans and Fred Clarke of the Pittsburgh Nationals. Unfortunately, there was not a Honus Wagner, Tris Speaker, or Leslie Bush to be found.

In frustration, Julie wrote a letter to the company asking if she could be sent the three missing cards. (She decided *not* to add a suggestion that there be more peanuts in each box.) She received a relatively quick but, alas, disappointing response. The letter politely stated that it would not be fair to the collectors of their toys and cards if obtaining such items was as simple as writing and asking for them. As an act of good will, the company provided her with a fifty cent coupon good on her next purchase and a print-out listing fellow card collectors with whom she might be able to negotiate a trade.

Rather than giving up our quest for the last three cards, we not only used the coupon but also kept buying and eating more. Larry was thrilled when, after 90 boxes, he finally got Honus Wagner. Unfortunately, almost every card for the next six boxes was—you guessed it—Honus Wagner. Tris Speaker arrived just before we left for Cape Cod for our annual vacation. We now needed one more card: Leslie Bush.

My hope that our vacation would include a respite from the snack was not answered. The day we arrived at our rented cottage at the Cape, I unpacked while the rest of my family headed out to pick up groceries. They came back with a week's supply of food and a two-week supply of the snack.

Then three days into our vacation, while Larry was on a day trip to Nantucket with a friend, Adam opened a box and found the elusive Leslie Bush. Three months and 138 boxes into our mission, our collection was complete.

We were still not done. Larry realized that with so many duplicates, we were only a few cards short of two complete sets. It took another two weeks—twenty-one boxes—to complete the search.

Our family still reminisces about the summer of 1993 and our quest to find the elusive Leslie Bush. Even today, when we head to a spring training game or even a regular season match-up, Larry will buy the familiar red, silver, and blue box to get into the spirit of the game. I, for one, settle for the peanuts.

TEN

The Mother Who Was Out in Left Field On a Field Trip

When my daughter was in sixth grade, I committed one of the most serious forms of child abuse that a mother could inflict on her child. I volunteered to chaperone one of Julie's field trips.

Before you demand that I lose custody of my children for this crime, I wish to plead innocence due to ignorance. How was I supposed to know that, for a twelve-year-old, having a mother along on a class trip was more embarrassing than a case of adolescent acne?

The last time I had signed up for such an excursion was Julie's first grade trip to the Rensselaer Museum. At that point in her life, Julie was thrilled to have me accompany her. She held my hand all afternoon, showed me off to all her friends, and insisted that I sit next to her on the bus.

I should have known that twelve is not six. When my son Adam was the same age, I drove him to Clifton Country Mall to buy clothes for school "Look, Mom, I know you have to come along because you drive and I don't," he said. "But walk ten feet behind me and, no matter what you do, don't *LOOK* like me!"

Julie had obviously adopted the same attitude. Not-so-subtle signs had been evident for some time. She had been increasingly critical of me. A sneeze, a joke, a comment to my friend were all viewed as attempts to humiliate her in front of others.

With this in mind, when the notice about the field trip to Higgins Armory in Worcester, Massachusetts, came home from Okte Elementary, I made sure to ask Julie if she actually wanted me to go. She gave me a quick, "If you want to," which I took for consent. I sent in a note to the teacher and submitted a request for personal time from my job. Within a day after I signed up, Julie used every opportunity to tell me how I should conduct myself during the five hour round trip on the bus and the time spent at the Higgins Armory.

As a public service to any parent who has decided—as I did —to spend a day 'bonding' with his/her child by signing up to help chaperone a field trip, I share these caveats:

Rule One: Dress conservatively. No loud print shirts, no dorky hats, no ridiculous fanny packs, no stupid shoes. The best route is to have your child pick out an outfit at least three days before the trip so that he or she can be assured that your clothing choice is appropriate.

Rule Two: On the bus ride to and from the destination, be as unobtrusive as possible. Sit far away from your child, preferably on another bus. If the children sing songs they have learned in chorus, do not join in. Parents have voices that are either too loud, too high, or too off-key.

Rule Three: Do not communicate through words or gestures with your child. Do not under any circumstances acknowledge that you have any relationship with him or her for the entire day. The only exception to this rule is if and when he or she needs money.

Rule Four: Do not talk to your child's friends. It does not matter that some of these children may live under your roof as much as your own offspring. Speaking to them smacks of familiarity.

Rule Five: Do not talk to other parents. This could possibly lead to discussing your child or your child's friends.

Rule Six: Do not ask anyone for directions to the public bathroom. Better yet, do not even go to the bathroom. The fact that such needs exist is a sure sign that you are human, a condition that cannot be tolerated by a twelve-year-old.

Rule Seven: Do not eat or drink for the entire time you are on the trip. First of all, you may spill a drink or get crumbs on the front of the outfit that your child so carefully selected. Furthermore, food and drink causes you to go to the bathroom, a direct violation of Rule Six.

Rule Eight: Avoid any mannerisms or idiosyncrasies that will embarrass your child. These include talking to yourself, humming mindlessly, biting your nails, scratching body parts, blowing your nose, sneezing, coughing, walking, sitting, and/or breathing.

Rule Nine: Do not express an opinion on any aspect of the field trip. For example, do not comment on the beauty of a painting, the interesting design of a chair, or the intricate details of a sculpture. This shows you have personal tastes, which are invariably the direct opposite of those of your child.

After hearing all my daughter's concerns, I offered to back out. With the field trip less than a week away, however, Julie felt as I did: A commitment was a commitment.

"Why did you agree to my going in the first place?" I asked.

"I didn't want to hurt your feelings," she said. "Besides, I think you'll have a good time."

"Thanks, hon," I said. "I'm glad you're thinking of your mother."

ELEVEN

The Dog Who Ate the Blintzes and Other Tales of Canine Woes

Living in the big, old Victorian house in Keeseville, my parents, my three siblings and I always had pets. The first cat came with the moving van. My father warned my mother that the dark, dirty pantry was infested with mice. Fluffy must have had a field day that first year until the kitchen was remodeled. Fluffy was followed by many other cats, several goldfish, a few turtles, and number of tropical fish in a huge aquarium in the dining room. None of these pets created anywhere near the chaos that our few canines did over the years.

My father had this vision of owning a dog that fit into the romanticized version glorified by Lassie and Rin Tin Tin. For this reason, he interspersed moments of sanity by surprising my mother and us children with a dog. Today, people who obtain a dog immediately enroll themselves and their pet in one of the numerous dog training classes available. This was, however, the 1960s. My father's expectation was that one of the children would take on the responsibility of reining in the exuberant, wild puppies he had brought home on a whim. Alas, none of us were effective Dog Whisperers or even dog trainers.

One of the first dogs brought into our house was a big, happy, untrained boxer named Penny. My father got an exceptional deal on her as she came undocked. Her long tail acted like a whip, knocking into everything in her wake and actually hurting people when she wagged it. One Shavuot, my mother decided to make a big batch of blintzes as we were having company. Blintzes are similar to French crepes, notoriously time consuming as each pancake is filled with a cheese, sugar, and egg mixture and then fried. She had completed the preparation of three dozen blintzes and had lined them up on clean white towels on the kitchen counter. She decided to finish up some laundry in the basement before frying them. When Mom came back fifteen minutes later, Penny had pulled the towels off the counter. The half-eaten blintzes were all over the kitchen floor, and the dog was having the feast of her life. Penny didn't have a chance after that, and my father had to find another home for the hapless dog.

Over the years, my father brought home a few other dogs that fared no better than Penny. One dog jumped up on everyone who came into the house. Another followed me to a friend's home, grabbed my coat between his teeth, and had a grand time playing tug of war with my jacket until someone managed to get him off me. A third dog frightened my mother so much with his barking and growling that she climbed up on the kitchen table and screamed until Dad rescued her.

The one dog that had any staying power was a beautiful but not especially bright Irish setter. My father, in his usual fashion, went out on a summer Sunday morning in 1968 to get the paper and came home with the adorable puppy. As I was leaving for college in two months, Dad and—surprisingly—Mom thought the dog would be good company for my younger sister. Bobbie named the dog Moose, after my brother's college nickname. Bobbie took good care of Moose until she left for college five years later. When Larry entered the picture in 1973, my future husband became the dog's new best friend. Moose wouldn't leave his side, and the two of them would go for long walks and runs together.

Moose had her share of adventures: She got skunked on more than one occasion, ate one of my brand new contact lenses when it fell out of my eye the first month I got them, and frequently grabbed food out of the hands of unsuspecting grandchildren.

One morning, we woke up to find that a herd of cows had strayed onto the lot next to my parents' cottage on Lake Champlain. Moose bolted out of the door, barking and chasing after them. The frightened cows began a stampede towards a neighbor's front sliding doors just as was she was opening the shades. Legend is that her screams are still echoing around Willsboro Bay.

Once Bobbie was out of the house, my parents found it difficult to take care of Moose and gave the dog to a family with children who lived on a farm. My parents actually missed her but were glad she had a place to run and play.

Although Larry's family had a series of well-behaved dogs when he was growing up, Larry and I have never owned a dog during our entire married life. My own history of dogs gone wild and my husband's accurate assessment that he would be the one walking it in rain, wind, and minus zero temperatures, resulted in our decision to limit pets to cats, turtles, and an occasional foster gerbil.

My mother once told me that she found it easier to raise four children than to take care of the motley collection of canines that came in and out of our house in Keeseville. "Perhaps," she once mused, "we would have done better if we had a Dr. Spock manual for dogs as we had for our children." Or, maybe, Mom, we Cohens just needed to stick with raising children and making blintzes in dog-free kitchens.

TWELVE

Where Was Freud When I Needed Him?

Some people don't remember their dreams. Mine are so vivid that they have become at times their own reality, creating some embarrassing moments.

When Larry and I first moved to Clifton Park in 1976, we didn't know anyone. At the urging of Larry's mom, a lifetime member of Hadassah, I joined the fairly new but very active Clifton Park chapter. The first meeting I attended, I sat with a group of women who were also newcomers to the community. We became friends, and several of us became pregnant the same year. We attended Lamaze classes together, went to each other's son's bris, and attended La Leche League meetings together. Yes, 1978 was a bumper year for Clifton Park Hadassah babies.

When my son Adam was around eighteen months old, that core of Hadassah mothers, along with a few other friends, formed a playgroup for our children. Each week, we would take turns dropping off our child with the designated mother at ten o'clock in the morning. Seven of us would go off on our merry way, free from toddler responsibilities for two blissful hours. The assigned mother would organize activities for the day's playgroup. During the winter months, the children played with toys, participated in an arts and crafts project, or enjoyed a story time. In the summer, the children went outside and played on the swing sets or in sandboxes. The mom-in-charge fed the children lunch—usually peanut butter and jelly sandwiches, fruit juice and cookies. By twelve noon, the playgroup mom was more than ready to hand the visiting children back to their own mothers.

The group functioned smoothly, and the children, for the most part, played well together. Yes, there were the expected outbursts and tantrums and fights. But this arrangement worked well for both the children and the mothers.

The eight of us became good friends, so I was saddened to hear that Fern, her husband Steve, and their son Marshall were moving to Chicago. I shared the news with my friend Diane during a phone call on a non-playgroup day.

Diane immediately questioned my information. "Are you sure?" she said. "I spoke to Fern yesterday, and she didn't mention anything about a move."

"No," I insisted. "Steve got a promotion with his company. Fern feels bad about leaving all her friends here, but she said this is an excellent opportunity for Steve. They are moving in two months."

Diane was still doubtful. "Look, I have three-way calling on my phone. Let me get hold of Fern right now and the three of us can talk."

I agreed and heard a few clicks and buzzes as Diane set up the conference call. We soon heard Fern's hello.

"Hi Fern!" said Diane. "Marilyn was telling me that you are moving to Chicago!"

"I'm not moving to Chicago," Fern immediately responded. "Where did you hear that, Marilyn?"

"We talked yesterday," I responded. "You told me all about Steve's promotion and his transfer."

"What promotion?" Fern said. "As far as I know, we are staying put in Clifton Park."

It was just at that moment that the circumstances of my "conversation" with Fern fell into place. Horrified, I realized that this entire episode had taken place in a dream I had experienced the night before. Every moment of that now-nightmare came rushing back to me.

"Oh my G-d!" I exclaimed. "I am so very sorry! This whole conversation took place in my sleep!"

I was totally embarrassed. I stuttered my way through apologies to both Fern and Diane. They understood—as much as they could understand that this crazy lady couldn't distinguish dreams from reality. And what if Fern thought it was 'wishful thinking'?

All of the mothers in that playgroup remained friends through our children's nursery school and the years that followed. Three years later, some of us mothers, who all delivered younger siblings in 1981, formed another playgroup with the same positive results.

Many of us joined the same synagogue. Even after some moved out of the area, we continued to stay in touch. We attended each other's children's bar and bat mitzvahs, rejoiced in their successes in high school and college, comforted each other during the sad times, and shared each other's joy in our former toddlers' marriages and the births of each other's grandchildren. Obviously, Fern and her family didn't move to Chicago. She and Steve still live in the same house that housed our sons' playgroup over thirty-five years ago. She is currently president of Sisterhood and is stepping up to the plate to become the next president of Congregation Beth Shalom.

I still clearly remember the "conversation" I had with Fern. After that incident, I was a little more careful after waking up from a vivid dream. I have checked myself several times over the years, realizing that I was about to pull another "Fern Moment." But I also remember our playgroup and the friendships that grew from those once-a-week get-togethers.

THIRTEEN

What Should I Wear to School?

Every August, newspapers are loaded with advertisements for back-to-school clothes. Viewing the options is an experience for me: lacy tight tops, skinny jeans, and leggings for the girls; tee shirts and jeans for the boys. The choices are a far cry from what I wore to school in the fifties and sixties.

I can still remember the smell and feel of new clothes that I put on for elementary school. I always got a couple of new dresses, sweet cotton prints with Peter Pan collars worn with white anklets and sturdy Mary Janes. Since my September birthday always fell close to school opening, new school clothes were included in my presents. I felt a little cheated, as my siblings and friends were getting new clothes, and it wasn't even their birthday.

By the time I entered junior high, I became more interested in fashion and studied *Seventeen* magazine all summer, admiring the "mod" look popularized by Twiggy and Jean Shrimpton. Upstate New York was not exactly the fashion capital of the world, but I tried. My stand-by outfit in the mid-sixties was a solid a-line skirt with a ribbed or "poor boy" sweater; a jumper with a turtle neck, or a blouse and a pair of 'skorts,' a skirt/pant combination. However, my favorite outfit was a short sleeve wool 'Mod' dress, orange with a white hem and white stripes running horizontally down each side. When I wore it, I felt as if I were one of those beautiful, skinny models.

Skorts were the closest I got to pants, as girls were not allowed to wear slacks to our school. My sister Laura and a group of her friends were sent home in their senior year, 1960, when they all came dressed in pants. This all changed in 1966 when one of Larry's classmates at Saratoga Springs High School was sent home for "improper attire" when she wore slacks to school on a cold winter's day. The school's Board of Education decision was overturned by New York State Commissioner of Education, James Allen, who ruled in the student's favor, freeing female students across the state to forgo dresses and skirts for the comfort of pants. Of course, what we wore, the tailored solid or tweed woolen styles of the 1960s, is a far cry from the leggings and torn jeans that are so popular now.

Once I had children, my job was to shop for them. Dressing Adam for kindergarten was easy. I got a number of Healthtex polo shirts and pant sets from Larry's parents' store in Schuylerville, and Adam was perfectly happy. As he got older, Adam switched to jeans and superhero or Star Wars tee shirts.

Then came Julie. Getting her dressed for school became a major battle each morning, especially in first grade. Over the summer, I had taken her clothing shopping, and we had selected several new outfits. When school started, however, she complained that nothing felt comfortable. Her preferred but limited wardrobe came down to one turquoise tee shirt with an imprint of three dancing cats on the front; two pairs of leggings, white with silver metallic stars in the fabric; two pairs of frayed and graying white socks with holes in the toes; and one pair of worn pink sneakers with ratty shoelaces. We fought every morning for several weeks. I finally gave in as it wasn't worth the time and energy. Every night, once she went to bed, I would wash and dry her "kitty cat" outfit, and every morning she put it back on. She wore that shabby outfit almost every day for an entire year.

When Larry and I went in for a teacher's conference in the spring,

I felt I had to apologize. "Honestly, Julie *has* other clothes, but she chooses not to wear them," I explained. "Julie wears the same outfit every day because she is comfortable in it. I wash them every night, so she is always clean." Julie's teacher smiled and said that was common with first and second graders. Julie also hated to be warm, and she wore an unzipped light winter coat, usually with no hat and gloves, down to the bus, even if it was bitter cold outside. I finally gave up on that battle as well, deciding that she was smart enough to figure out if she needed to add extra layers.

Because of my experience with Julie, I've learned to appreciate outfits worn by other young children. When I see, for example, a little girl wearing a flowered top, plaid pants, a pink tutu overskirt, polka dot rain boots, and a tiara for good measure, I ask her if she picked out her own clothes and then compliment her on her good taste. My favorite picture of my great nephew captured his three-year-old self sitting in his car seat on the way to swim practice with his swim suit, his Spiderman pajama top, and cowboy boots. Guess who picked out his outfit for that day?

To this day, Julie hates the heat. She lives in Colorado at 9100 feet, where it could snow nine to ten months a year. Yes, she is happy as a big horn sheep living in the mountains. To her credit, however, she has become a sharp dresser. Now when I visit her, she takes *me* clothes shopping, and I am happy with her suggestions. And, thankfully, not one of her choices has included dancing kitties or white leggings with silver metallic stars.

FOURTEEN

Going Home Again: The Next Generation
Takes Over the Old Homestead

Thomas Wolfe famously stated, "You can never go home again." Larry's sister and brother-in-law are living proof that one should *never* say never.

When he returned from military service after the Korean War, Larry's father Ernie collected Doris and their two children Anita and Larry from Bubbe Rose's house in Syracuse. They moved into an older house on Avery Street in Saratoga Springs. By the mid-sixties, the family had expanded to include Marilyn Pearl and Carole. Mom and Dad decided to build a new house less than a mile away on Iroquois Drive.

When construction was finished in July 1964, Anita was already away at college in Rochester. Larry, who missed the old house and neighborhood, lived in the new house for only eighteen months before he headed to college in Boston. Marilyn Pearl and Carole were young enough to adjust quickly to the move and, in retrospect, to live enough years at Iroquois Drive to create many happy childhood memories. Dad loved the oversized two car garage that held his tools, a large workbench, and his golf clubs, and the family room that had a section for a regulation sized pool table.

It was Mom, however, who was most excited about her "dream" house. She loved the new kitchen with its ample cabinets. As she hated the heat, she appreciated the central air conditioning. Her mahogany table and buffet, which barely squeezed into the house on Avery Street, worked well in the new dining room. A large cabinet displayed her crystal and china, and the living room was large enough to hold an oversized couch, several chairs, tables, and a piano. Mom took a great deal of pride in her new home, and it showed. She was a meticulous housekeeper, and it was rare to see anything out of place or cluttered. Every tabletop shined, the floors were polished, the carpets were vacuumed, the closets and drawers were organized, the bathrooms gleamed; the laundry and storage rooms were spotless. Even though she employed outside help, she was known to clean before and after her cleaning lady. As a matter of fact, one of our favorite 'Doris' stories is that Mom scrubbed her kitchen sink so vigorously that she literally wore a hole through the porcelain.

In addition, Mom was an outstanding cook and baker. She enjoyed having her children, grandchildren, friends, and out-of-town relatives to her house whenever she had the opportunity. She often spent the weeks before major Jewish holidays planning her menu, cooking, baking, and freezing much of the food in preparation. Once the holiday arrived, she would open up the dining room table to its full length, put on her freshly ironed table cloths, and set it with her best china and crystal. At her dinners the table would be laden with her specialties: brisket on Rosh Hashanah, tongue and chopped eggplant at the Yom Kippur Break-the Fast, and matzoh ball soup and roasted chicken on Passover. When the dinner was over, Mom insisted on doing the dishes. "No one can do them as well as I can," she would say as she shooed us out of the kitchen. As she got older, we worried that all her cooking and cleaning was too much for her. She brushed off our concerns, saying she loved to entertain. We knew better than to argue with Doris Shapiro.

After they retired, Mom and Dad spent part of the winter in Florida in a condo. Dad loved the sunshine, the pool, the golf courses, and the activities. Mom, however, missed her friends and her home in Saratoga Springs. When I visited her in early April 1994, she was already packing up, looking forward to returning to her beloved home on Iroquois Drive, and getting ready for the Passover seder.

She never made it home. On the way up north, while visiting Carole and her family in Charleston, South Carolina, Mom had a heart attack. She passed away during open heart surgery on April 26, 1994. Dad was devastated by the loss of his beloved Doris. He himself had to have open heart surgery that summer. When he died on December 20, the doctor said that Dad had succumbed not from cardiac disease but from a broken heart.

After Dad's funeral, their beautiful home sat empty and quiet. It seemed as if the house, as well as the family, was in mourning. We initially discussed cleaning it out and putting it up for sale. The grief was still too raw to put these thoughts into action.

Fortunately, the house never had to go on the market. After many years of living all over the country, Carole's husband Bill was to retire from the Navy in June 1996. Throughout the years, they had always said how much they missed being close to the family. With Mom and Dad gone, they were even more certain that their hearts and lives belonged in Saratoga Springs. They had the perfect solution: They would buy the house from the estate and move from Charleston, South Carolina, to Iroquois Drive.

Eighteen months after Dad's passing, the Leakakos family pulled into the driveway. On that beautiful June afternoon, even the house seemed to be smiling. That first summer, the four siblings and their spouses amicably divided up the contents. Some were designated by Mom through handwritten notes; some were chosen by each for sentimental reasons. Then it fell to Carole and Bill to figure out what to do with the remainder of the contents. Mom and Dad had accumulated much over their thirty years in the house. Many of the duplicated and unwanted items were given to local charities. The outdated or unusable were tossed in a dumpster. Within a year, Mom and Dad's cold, vacant house became the warm, welcoming Leakakos home. The four people and one dog settled comfortably into their new residence.

We all agreed that Mom must have rolled over in her grave when her house, her pride and joy, changed hands. Mom may have been a meticulous housekeeper, but Carole, by her own admission, did not follow in her footsteps. Her style was more "I have two active boys and a dog that sheds" casual. Truthfully, the house seemed a *little* crowded for quite a while. Carole and Bill had brought their own furniture, but they had difficulty parting with much of the original furniture her parents had purchased. While moving around the country, Carole had also collected crafts and treasures which filled any remaining nooks and crannies. Not surprisingly, no one cared that the house was not up to the old standards as long as the house was again filled with the Shapiro family parties.

And frequently, it is. Carole may not have inherited her mother's insistence for an immaculately clean home. However, she did inherit her mother's love of entertaining. She and Bill have continued the tradition of making Iroquois Drive the center for family gatherings, birthday and graduation parties, and holiday dinners. Their Passover seders are epic: they have had up to thirty-five people in attendance. People are seated not only around the mahogany dining room table but also at card tables and chairs brought by the guests. The china and crystal and linens have been replaced with paper plates, disposable silverware, and plastic tablecloths, but no one minds. Friends and family bring their own specialties to share, and everyone shares in the clean-up. Carole and Bill are excellent hosts—welcoming, relaxed, gracious.

So, Mr. Wolfe, you *can* go home again. And to my dear Carole and Bill, we are glad you did.

FIFTEEN

My Dad: The Designated Driver

A Father's Day memory: It is 1956. My father is sitting behind the steering wheel of an idling sedan in the driveway of our house in Keeseville. Laura, Jay, and I are squirming in the back seat. Dad is smoking a Kent and listening to a baseball game on the radio. He gives the horn an impatient tap to hurry along my mother, who is inside the house diapering Bobbie and pulling together last minute items for our car trip. He honks again, more loudly. "Where is that woman?" he asks. "We're going to be late."

For over sixty-five years, my father was our family's self-appointed Designated Driver. Born and raised in Queens, my father learned how to drive when he was fifteen years old at his grandfather's farm in Burlington, Vermont. In 1940, my mother took her place in the passenger seat. By 1955, four children were filling up the remaining space.

Out of financial necessity, our family usually owned "gently used" cars. No matter how pristine they were when purchased, each vehicle soon lost the 'new-car' feel once our huge family—with an occasional dog along for the ride—took ownership.

These were the days before cars had safety features. No one wore seat belts; babies sat on mothers' laps; Dad's extended right arm held us back when we were forced to a sudden stop.

As the family grew, sedans gave way to station wagons. One or two of us children happily climbed into the back, where we bounced our way to a school function or the beach or a relative's house or even to visits to our grandparents in New York City, oblivious to any danger. Fortunately, Dad was an excellent driver. He was never involved in an accident. And his only speeding ticket was when—as he never let me forget—he was rushing home from a trip to Plattsburgh after I was car sick.

Not that he wasn't guilty of "pedal to the metal." In the 1960s, my father was elected coroner of Essex County, New York, a position he held for over twenty years. When he got the call from the state police that he was needed to investigate an unattended or suspicious death, Dad would rush out to his car, put the Essex County Coroner sign in his window, slap on his "Kojak" flasher on top of the roof, and drive to the scene like a bat out of hell. If the call came in the middle of the night, one of us would often ride with Dad to keep him company. I remember sitting in the passenger seat while Dad careened through the back roads of Reber or Willsboro or Port Kent, praying one of the other three coroners in the county wouldn't have to investigate *our* untimely demise.

Soon after they retired in 1981, Dad and Mom began spending half the year in Florida. Each year in mid-October, they drove the 1500 miles to their condo in Lauderdale Lakes. The week before Memorial Day, they took the same route back. Although they eventually took the auto train to reduce driving time, Dad continued his reign as exclusive—and excellent—driver.

As he got into his eighties, however, his driving skills declined. His hearing was poor, his reaction times were slow, and he relied too often on cruise control so he wouldn't have to regulate the gas pedal. Concrete car stop bumpers in parking lots saved many an eating place from becoming an impromptu drive-in restaurant. Still, Dad insisted on taking the wheel, promising to limit his trips to nearby restaurants and stores.

In 2005, while visiting Mom and Dad in Florida, Jay and his wife

Leslie made plans for the four of them to go out to dinner. The usual fight ensued. "I'll drive!" Jay offered. "Absolutely not," Dad countered "You're my guest. *I'll* drive."

The route to the restaurant included a section on a multi-lane expressway. Dad was in the far left lane when he suddenly crossed four lanes to get to the exit ramp. "We watched in horror from the back seat," Jay said. "Fifteen years later, I can still remember how Leslie's nails felt as she dug them into my arm until I bled."

After that incident, we children insisted Dad give up the car. We arranged for Mom and Dad to move into Coburg Village, an independent living facility near Larry and me that offered among other amenities transportation to stores and doctors' offices. They flew up to their new home, and Laura and Jay drove Dad's car to our house. Dad's Toyota would stay safely in our driveway until Julie picked it up and drove it back to Colorado that summer.

For the next few months, Dad complained incessantly about how we had taken away his independence. The day Julie came home to claim the Toyota, however, Dad pulled out of his wallet the registration AND an extra car key.

"You could have walked down the driveway and driven that car anytime you wanted to!" I said.

"I know," he said with a wink.

After that, Dad grudgingly accepted his place in the front passenger seat when either Larry or I drove. Six months before he passed away, Dad got a brand new shiny red mobility scooter. When I came over to have dinner that night in the Coburg dining room, Dad was already sitting on his new toy with a huge smile on his face. Mom and I followed him as he navigated his way down the long hallway to the open elevator door. Entering a little too fast, he gently hit the back wall. "I'm fine!" Dad said with a wink. "I got this!"

Of course he was fine! My father was finally in the driver's seat again.

SIXTEEN

So Many Books, So Little Time

Shortly after my parents were married, their first argument was about reading. With an $18-a-week income as a sales clerk in Alburgh, Vermont, my father was spending up to $4 a week on magazines and books. My mother managed to curb his spending, but neither curbed their love for the written word.

My parents were first-generation Americans, born of Jewish Russian immigrants. Children of the Depression, economic reality squelched any hopes for education beyond high school. My parents compensated for their lack of opportunity with a legacy of literature: books, magazines, newspapers, and frequent trips to the libraries in the small towns in Vermont and upstate New York where they raised their four children.

As a result, my siblings and I grew up in a house full of books. Two rooms had floor-to-ceiling shelves loaded with novels, second-hand encyclopedias, and American Heritage anthologies. I remember sitting on my mother's lap as she read Golden Books to me. Birthdays and holidays always meant new books: *The Wizard of Oz*, Shirley Temple's *Story Book*, and, in later years, the latest Nancy Drew mystery which my father would purchase in New York City on his business trips.

When the books in our house weren't enough, I walked to the small but well-stocked library around the corner from our house in

Keeseville. An early reader, I soon graduated from the six-foot bookshelf stuffed with picture books like *The Cat in the Hat* and *Curious George* and moved onto the twelve-foot high shelves with more challenging books. *Pippi Longstocking* and *Alice in Wonderland* were followed by Helen Keller's autobiography and *The Good Earth*. I would spend hot, summer afternoons in a green lounge chair on the side porch doing what I loved best—reading.

It was no surprise, then, that my four years of college focused on literature. I spent hours reading, discussing, and analyzing Shakespeare, Milton, Melville, and Hemingway. My literature courses were not work. They were an academic extension of those leisurely afternoons in the green lounge chair.

When I met Larry, one of the first qualities we found that we had in common was our interest in reading. His first gift to me was a copy of Paul Gallico's *The Snow Goose*; my first gift to him was Thoreau's *Cape Cod*.

As our parents did before us, Larry and I passed this legacy on to our own children. Bedtime was always a time for us to introduce them to our childhood friends—Francis the Badger, Amelia Bedelia, and Ramona the Brave—and meet new ones, including the Berenstein Bears, Corduroy, and Sylvester and his magic pebble. Books filled their shelves, and they got library cards as soon as they could write their own names. Adam became immersed in Tolkien and C. S. Lewis; Julie in L. M. Montgomery's *Anne of Green Gables* series and Jane Austen. Our conversations with our children still include discussions of books we are reading.

Those conversations have also been with friends. For thirty-four years, I was a member of a monthly book club in Upstate New York. The members of the group changed over the years as people moved away or had other commitments. The format, however, remained the same. Taking turns meeting in each other's homes, we spent the first half hour socializing in the living room. We then moved to the dining room, where we discussed future book recommendations and scheduling over beverages and too many desserts—at least one had to have chocolate— candy, nuts, and fruit. Then we began our discussion about the pre-determined book of the month.

The fiction and non-fiction we read reflected the stages of our lives. Books on raising children gave way to those on balancing work and family to dealing with aging parents to our own retirements. We often chose best-selling and/or critically acclaimed fiction and non-fiction. With some help from discussion questions from Reading Group Guides, the group took time to weigh in on our opinion of the selection. We all loved Ann Patchett's *Bel Canto*; we all struggled through Annie Proulx's *Shipping News*.

Elizabeth Gilbert's *Eat, Pray, Love* literally split the table: One side thought the author was an irresponsible witch; the other side admired her independence and courage.

The means with which we read our selections also evolved over the years. The hardcover and paperback books were replaced with audio books and electronic readers. My personal favorite, a reflection of my aging eyes, was anything in large print. No matter what the selection or the means, the discussions were lively, the food was plentiful, and the pleasure of spending an evening with fellow readers was immeasurable. Once I retired, I doubled my pleasure by joining Clifton Park's Hadassah Book Club.

Saying good-bye to my book clubs when I moved to Florida was one of my hardest tasks. Not surprisingly, I immediately joined a new book club. The women in Book Babes have helped make my transition to Florida easier, as I again enjoying the company of bright, articulate women who love to read and to discuss good literature.

Dr. Seuss wrote, "The more that you read, the more things you will know. The more that you learn, the more places you'll go." So hundreds, maybe thousands of books later, I continue to grow from the legacy that was given to me by my parents and that I have shared with my family and friends. So many books, so little time! But what a good time I am having.

SEVENTEEN

The Best Gifts Ever: Pianos and Music Changed Our Lives

For our family, three of the best gifts we ever received were an ugly orange spinet, a mahogany baby grand, and a walnut Yamaha upright.

After the war, my parents and my two older siblings moved from New London, Connecticut, to Potsdam, New York, so that my father could help Uncle Eli, my mother's brother, with his clothing business. Housing was difficult to find in 1948, and my parents were left no option but to purchase a small ranch house on top of a frequently windy hill. Cramming the four of them into the two-bedroom house was difficult enough. When I arrived in 1950, things got even more crowded. The kitchen was so small that the person sitting in the kitchen chair nearest to the refrigerator would have to stand up if someone had to grab the milk. Laura and Jay shared a bedroom, and my crib was sandwiched into my parents' bedroom. The tiny living room had a couch, two chairs, my playpen, toys, books, and, in time, an ugly piano that was one of my sister's best gifts.

Potsdam was home to the state college, which included the Crane School of Music, This provided many musical opportunities to the community. Laura walked past Crane on her way home from school every day and heard the students practicing their instruments. Intrigued and inspired, she asked my parents for a piano. After proving herself by taking lessons using the neighbor's rickety spinet, she got her wish. My parents purchased an old upright painted a hideous butterscotch orange that barely fit into the already full living room. The tiny house often reverberated with music, especially when friends gathered around the piano. Uncle Eli, who could not read music, played any requested song by ear, so he often was on the piano bench.

In 1952, my father took a job in Keeseville, New York, managing a Pearl's department store, one of several in a chain owned by my great-uncle Paul. In order to save money, my parents hired a couple of men from Pearl's to pack up the household belongings into the company truck and safely deliver them to our new home. Unfortunately, the men dropped the piano while unloading it. The instrument, never in tune to start, was now hopelessly flat with a few more non-functional keys. That didn't stop us from playing. My older siblings and I took lessons with varying degrees of mediocrity. We mixed our John Thompson piano lesson books with more popular sheet music, including such Fifties hits as "Stranger on the Shore" and "Mack the Knife." Laura's and my favorites were from the American Songbook. We had a healthy collection of Rodgers and Hammerstein, Cole Porter, and George Gershwin.

By the age of twelve, I had gone through a couple of piano teachers, one who retired and one who moved away. Despite the lack of lessons, innate talent, and a decent instrument, I still loved to play. I began lobbying for a new piano. I knew, however, that getting even another second-hand one that was in a little better shape than our orange relic was probably out of financial reach for our family.

One evening before Chanukah in 1962, my parents called me into the kitchen. That afternoon, my father learned that one of his customers was moving to a smaller home and was selling a used baby grand for only five hundred dollars. Was my father interested? Yes, he was, and I was getting my wish. I cried for joy, even more so when the beautiful instrument with its shiny mahogany finish was delivered later that week. Unlike our tiny box of a house in Potsdam, our Victorian house in Keeseville had enough room for the baby grand. With a minimal rearrangement of furniture, the piano became the centerpiece of our living room.

That January, I started lessons with the young new Keeseville Central School music teacher. Initially, I was humiliated to find out that I needed to start from the beginning level books to improve my skills. Over the next three years, I managed to work my way through the third level of the John Thompson series. My teacher, knowing my love for the movie and Broadway show tunes, also supplemented the classics with more contemporary selections such as "Sunrise, Sunset" from *Fiddler on the Roof*, "You'll Never Walk Alone" from *Carousel,* and, my favorite, "Moon River."

The piano again became a gathering place for family and friends. I often played while my sisters sang along. My brother even joined in with his trombone. I missed lots of the notes, my sisters were not known for their vocal talents, and my brother was no Trombone Shorty, but we loved the chance to be together. My Grandpa Joe played Yiddish songs after he moved in with us after my grandmother's passing in 1966. Uncle Eli got to hammer out his share of songs when he visited us from Potsdam.

Once I left for college, I played infrequently, mostly on school breaks. When my parents moved out of their big house in Keeseville in 1982, the piano was sold as none of the children had room for it in their homes. Before my parents downsized, I collected all the sheet music from the house and stored it in our home "just in case" we ever got a piano.

After my daughter Julie was born, I was home with two small children. The days were getting long. Knowing how much I loved my baby grand in Keeseville, Larry encouraged me to look for a piano that would fit into our home. The Yamaha upright I selected from Clark

Music in Latham was delivered two weeks before my thirty-second birthday. I now put to use the sheet music my family and I had accumulated since my sister started lessons in Potsdam many years before. I spent many hours playing the piano, both for enjoyment and for the peace and serenity it gave me.

When she was a junior in high school, Julie decided to take piano lessons for the first time. I felt my musical life had come full circle when my daughter's teacher recommended we purchase new, unmarked John Thompson lesson books. At her first and only piano recital, Julie chose Pachebel's Canon and my old favorite, "Moon River."

When Larry and I decided to move, I initially thought of selling the piano. I rationalized that it was too expensive to ship to Florida; I didn't play *that* often; I could always use the piano in the community center a mile from our house. It was Larry who insisted that we pay the moving company to bring the piano with the rest of our household. There was no repeat of the Potsdam debacle. The piano arrived safely in our new home. From the moment I first touched the keys, I knew that we had made the right decision to move the Yamaha into our new home.

Soon after we moved in, I had three couples over for a Shabbat dinner. After dessert, my friend Becky, who taught music in high schools for many years, started looking at my sheet music collection. "This is fabulous!" she commented. "Please play for us!" Not used to an audience, I played hesitantly for a few songs, then Becky graciously took over the keyboard. For the next hour, we belted out songs from *Les Mis* and *Wicked* as well as my old favorites, "Sunrise, Sunset" and "Moon River." I had tears running down my cheeks from happiness. Thanks to my piano, our new home was filled with the sound of music.

EIGHTEEN

Young for Your Age: Facing Up to Getting Older

"To me, old age is fifteen years older than I am." wrote Bernard Baruch. As I work my way through my mid-sixties, I more fully appreciate the veracity of his wise quote.

I always have ignored my chronological age. I exercise daily, don't smoke, drink in moderation, and eat a healthy diet. According to my doctor, my medical stats are of those of a twenty-year old. By the grace of God, I inherited my mother's genes, which has rewarded me with a not a streak of grey in my full head of brown hair. People always tell me "You look so young for your age."

Umm. "Young for your age." I guess that means that my age usually *doesn't* look so young. But when I earnestly think about it, when was the last time anyone asked for my license to see if I were old enough to buy that bottle of Zinfandel at the liquor store? As a matter of fact, when was the last time I requested a senior ticket at the movie theater and the young clerk on the other side of the window responded, "Are you kidding me? There is no way you are a day over forty!"

The first time I ever realized that I was inching up there was when I was sixty years old and riding my bicycle on the Cape Cod Rail Trail. Three teenage boys who were stopped on the side of the path suddenly hurled themselves on their bikes and cut narrowly in front of me, almost causing a crash. I yelled out some appropriate but unprintable remark. One of them yelled back, "Get off the bike path, Old Lady!" I looked around to locate the octogenarian to whom they were referring. My goodness! They were talking about ME! Since when was I an "old lady"? Sixty may be the new forty, but for people under forty, I was— in fact—old.

The above is not to say that I myself did not perpetuate age discrimination in my younger years. When I was home for a college break, my mother told me that a couple they knew were getting a divorce after forty years of marriage. "Why would people that old get a divorce?" I commented. "Why bother when they have so few years left?"

When the last of my siblings headed out to college in 1975, my parents were in their mid-sixties. The four of us children commiserated long distance over the phone, wondering how our parents would survive the empty nest after raising children for thirty-three years. We pictured them sitting in their La-z-Boys, sadly rocking away, staring at the television set, and pining for the good old days. To our surprise, my mother quickly dropped twenty pounds and had her ears pierced. My father, who never cooked a meal in his life, started cooking gourmet dinners for the two of them. Yes—they were surviving nicely without us.

By the time I retired, the same attitude I had towards my parents was now being visited on me. When we were researching places in which to retire, I told my daughter about an active adult community in Colorado that looked promising. My one concern, I told Julie, was that the area was near where nuclear testing in the 1970s may have impacted the soil and water. "Mom, I wouldn't worry about it," Julie said. "At your age, you probably won't live long enough to feel the effects of radiation poisoning."

Soon after this humiliating exchange, my son echoed his sister's attitude. In our discussion about popular television shows, I mentioned that my seventy-something sister loved all the crime procedural shows—*Law and Order: SVU* and *Criminal Minds*. "Fits the targeted demographic," he commented. Trying to show how hip and young I was, I told him I prefer *The Big Bang Theory* and *Downton Abbey*. "Yes," Adam repeated. "Fits the same targeted demographic." As Sheldon on *The Big Bang Theory* would say, "Bazinga!"

So do we seniors, as Dylan Thomas wrote, "go gentle into that good night?" Hell, no! No longer encumbered with full-time jobs, my friends and family explore physical and intellectual pursuits. Like my parents, some lose weight and pierce their ears and learn how to cook gourmet meals. Others travel the country and the world in pursuit of learning. They look for birds. They climb forty-six Adirondack Peaks. They make beer and tend gardens. They patiently wait with their cameras until the sunlight is just right to get the perfect photograph. They raise money for charities by running and cycling long distances or jumping into freezing lakes. They take piano lessons and play the bassoon for community orchestras. They volunteer in nursing homes, on library and synagogue boards, in thrift shops, in schools. They coach Special Olympics. They become role models in courage as they battle and survive cancer and other life threatening illnesses. They fully embrace C. S. Lewis' philosophy, "You are never too old to set another goal or to dream a new dream."

Still, accepting that one is a senior does take adjustments. A few years ago, my family gathered in Connecticut to attend a cousin's Bat Mitzvah. A few weeks before the event, I reserved a block of five hotel rooms, using my AARP card to get a respectable discount. After the arrangements were made, I told my siblings to bring their own AARP cards so they could seal in the discounted price when they checked in. My younger sister, who was seven years beyond the necessary "fifty and older" membership requirement, told me she and her husband were not members of AARP because joining would make them feel old. Too bad, little sister. You are qualified, whether you like it or not.

NINETEEN

What's Your Resolution? The White Rabbit Vows to Be On Time!

"I'm late /I'm late /For a very important date./No time to say 'Hello, Goodbye'/I'm late, I'm late, I'm late." The White Rabbit

Lewis Carroll's classic *Alice in Wonderland* has always been one of my favorite children's books. I often dreamed of being Alice, falling down a rabbit hole, and meeting the Cheshire Cat and the Mad Hatter. A few years ago, however, I realized that that I wasn't Alice. I was the White Rabbit.

My epiphany came one Rosh Hashanah. My husband, who was unable to attend services due to a recent leg surgery, watched me from his recliner as I dashed around getting ready to leave at 10 o'clock in the morning, an hour after services began. "You're running late," he commented. "You seem to be doing that a lot lately."

Initially I was going to make some snide remark about spending time being "Nurse Nancy." Being the good wife, however, I bit my tongue and headed out the door.

As I spent time in synagogue that morning reflecting on my mad rush out the door, I realized that Larry was right. I was running behind schedule too often to count. I had left family and friends waiting at restaurants, movie theaters, and book stores. "I'm a little late!" I would announce breathlessly from my cell phone. "I should be there in ten or fifteen minutes." This had been going on long before Larry's surgery.

The irony in this situation is that I have always been known as the 'calendar queen.' For years, I lugged around a Franklin Planner, meticulously writing down every goal, task, and appointment. Respected by my boss and co-workers for my organizational skills, I was often given responsibility for event planning and implementation. My friends also recognized my strengths. For over twenty years, I was secretary of my book club. If anyone needed to know what book we were reading, or which member was hosting, or what date we were meeting, I was the person with the information.

Soon after I retired, I replaced the bulky Franklin planner with a smart phone that offered sophisticated—and addictive—time management tools to help me organize and plan every detail of my life. I drove Larry crazy with all the dings and beeps that signaled upcoming events. Unfortunately, all that electronic software didn't get me out the door any faster. To paraphrase Marilyn Monroe, "I've been *on* a calendar, but never on time!"

To be honest, I had better control of my time when I was teaching. For twenty-five years, I kept a strict classroom schedule, and I became impatient with the stragglers. It was when I moved out of the classroom into an administrative position that my ability was compromised.

My new job required that I wear many hats. I was responsible for public relations, institutional research, grant writing, special events, as well as any "duties as assigned." Although I enjoyed what I did, my job often required that I multitask. As a matter of fact, my boss felt strongly that the ability to juggle numerous balls in the air was a sign of a good administrator. As a result, I got into the habit of not only working on multiple projects at the same time but also switching quickly from one task to another. (Do you hear the sounds of all those balls I was trying to juggle bouncing?)

In order to handle the myriad of responsibilities, I found myself trying to squeeze 'one last thing' into my schedule. As a result, I often swept into meetings a couple of minutes late. Of course, since everyone I worked with was also under pressure to multitask, I was not always the last one in conference room. Larry also noticed it on the home front, as my desire to finish up an assigned project resulted in my arriving home one or two hours later than expected.

These bad habits carried into my personal life. Even after I retired, I still found myself trying to check off as many tasks on my to-do list as humanly possible. Whether it was calling to make a dentist appointment or folding the towels or sending an email to the children, I always was heading out the door at the last minute. Yes, I was like that proverbial White Rabbit whom I was emulating on that Rosh Hashanah morning.

I decided then and there that I would start the new year with the resolution to improve my track record for promptness. I would stop multi-tasking. No last minute phone calls. No last minute laundry folding. No more last minute communications. No, the new me would be showered, dressed, and ready ten minutes before any estimated time of departure, and I would leave for my destination with time to spare.

Or not. Despite my best intentions, it didn't always work out. I tried my best, but life kept getting in the way. A couple of months after I made my resolution, I was heading out the door to the YMCA around nine o'clock in the morning when my brother and sister-in-law called. We chatted until I begged off, saying I had to get out the door. Pulling the car out of the garage, I realized it had started snowing, which meant it took twice as long to make the four-mile trip. Once I got there, I ran into Tom, who caught me up on his winter running woes, and Linda, who shared with me that she was celebrating the holidays with her children from Chicago. Once I reached the elliptical, it took me about five minutes to untangle the wires on my ear buds—do they knot themselves every night to make me miserable? Three miles later, I turned off *West Side Story*, climbed off the stopped elliptical, and headed to Zumba. Sweating and breathless, I swooped into the exercise room two minutes before the instructor started class. At least I was on time. One woman showed up at twelve noon for our 11:30 a.m. Tuesday class, a feat I had pulled myself on a few occasions. Maybe she had an electronic calendar!

One of the advantages—or maybe disadvantages—of being Jewish is that twice a year we have opportunities to make resolutions: on our sacred Rosh Hashanah and on our secular New Year's Day. So, twice a year I resolve to continue working on the promise I made to myself that September—I would be on time. Whoops! Look at the clock! Need to stop editing this piece so I can make it to my 11:30 a.m. cardio-ballroom class....

TWENTY

Making the World a Better Place

In 2014, my husband Larry spent eight days in New Jersey as the New York State triathlon coach at the Special Olympics USA National Games. He described his experience as "incredible" and "life affirming." As soon as he arrived home, he tried to catch up on his sleep as he got less than five hours a night for the entire trip. How he got to this nirvana of sleep deprivation is part of Shapiro family lore.

Almost twenty years ago, Larry announced at the dinner table that he had signed the family up to volunteer at the New York State Special Olympics Summer Games that were being held at University of Albany in early June. My children had been involved in sports for several years, and Larry recognized that many volunteers had made their swimming, cross country, and track and field meets possible. He felt the four of us should pay it forward by contributing our time to the intellectually challenged athletes competing in track and field at the state-wide event.

We enjoyed our experience enough to sign up to volunteer again the following year. While at the games, Larry was asked to help out with the Saratoga County track and field program that met April through mid-June at the Saratoga Springs high school track. Soon after, Larry's co-worker also volunteered, and the two of them drove up every Monday and Thursday from downtown Albany. After a couple of years they extended their time commitment to include helping at local Special Olympic meets.

As the years progressed, Larry took on more and more responsibilities. He became head coach and held additional practices for athletes who exhibited high levels of skill in an event. He started a cross country running program, volunteered to coach for the Clifton Park bowling program, conducted coaching certification classes, and served on various Special Olympic committees. Larry knew that his involvement in Special Olympics would give him focus and purpose after he retired. It was shortly before his last day of work that he found out he was chosen as one New York State's track and field coaches for the National Games in Lincoln, Nebraska, in July 2010.

Along the way, Larry had convinced me and a number of friends to become track and field coaches, and we all gained much from our participation. The best part for all of us was being with the athletes at practices. Twice a week every spring, over forty athletes several coaches, and numerous parents and group home staff gathered at six o'clock at the track. Larry started everyone off with a team cheer P-A-C-E-R-S! Then the activities began. On the field, some athletes threw a softball while their distances were recorded by the coaches. A group of stronger athletes worked with a coach on the turbo-javelin and the shot-put. Others were practicing the standing long jump. On the track, athletes, depending on their levels and abilities, participated in runs, walks, and wheel chair events. The visually challenged ran twenty-five to fifty meters holding a baton strung through a 50-meter rope that was held in a straight line by cheering team mates. Practice ended with Larry gathering up the athletes for one more cheer before they went home. Two or three times a season, coaches and members of the team participated in local competitions. Whether we were at practices or at our meets, our athletes' times and distances were secondary to everyone enjoying themselves. The cheers were as loud for the athlete who threw the softball two meters as it was for the athlete who came in first in the 1500 meter run.

Larry took pride in the accomplishments of every athlete and was always recruiting new team members. While helping with Special Olympics bowling during fall 2013, Larry watched a young man decimate the pins with his powerful swing. Larry persuaded Rob to join track and field and use that strength to throw shot-put and the turbo javelin. By the end of his first season, the athlete impressed officials at the state games in Buffalo enough for him to be chosen to compete in Nationals in New Jersey. While there, Rob not only won a gold medal in his division in the shot-put but also came home with gold in the turbo javelin with the longest throw of anyone in the country.

Saying goodbye to the Pacers when we moved to Florida was one of our hardest moments. We follow their accomplishments on Facebook and through emails. In honor of our athletes, we have named the small body of water in our backyard "Pacers Pond."

Tikkun Olam is a Hebrew expression that means "repairing the world," the moral principal that states every individual should leave this world better than he or she found it. I take pride in knowing that Larry's involvement in Special Olympics is his way of making the world a better place for so many athletes.

TWENTY ONE

Is There Love After Retirement?

Ah! Young love! This is the time in life where two individuals cannot get enough of each other! Each moment away from one another is agony, and even when they are together in the same room, there is a desperate need to touch and hold and talk. Their wish is to share every waking moment together.

Yes, my husband and I were like that once. We met, we courted, we married, and we spent the next thirty-six years of our lives juggling our relationship with children, jobs, and outside commitments.

Then, Larry and I retired, and we got our wish. We were together twenty-four/seven, but we weren't young anymore. As a matter of fact, living under the same roof resulted in a period of major adjustment.

Please don't get me wrong. I love my husband dearly, and I am so grateful that we have had the opportunity to retire in good health. It is just that—well —love in the time of retirement may test even the closest relationship.

Our first battle took place soon after Larry retired. We were in the kitchen, cleaning up after dinner. As was our usual routine, Larry was putting away the leftovers while I was putting the dirty plates in the dishwasher. He looked over while he was closing the refrigerator door and offered, "Here, Marilyn, let me show you how to load a dishwasher."

I stopped mid-dish and stared at him. "What do you mean by that?"

"You're not doing it right. I can show you how to do it properly."

"So you mean to tell me I have been loading this thing WRONG for the last three decades?"

"Yes, my way is much more efficient!" We had a brief, spirited discussion as to whether he wanted to accept my tried and true way of doing it or if he wanted to wash dishes on his own for the rest of our married life. Thankfully, he saw it my way.

The second conflict occurred six months later when *I* retired. I planned to set up my calendar and some files in our home office. When I tried to find room on our computer desk, not an inch was available. "Larry," I said, "do you think you can organize all those piles on the desk so that we can share the space?"

"I retired first!" was his response. "I already claimed the desk. You will need to find another spot."

Initially, I managed to carve out a few inches of blank oak, but it wasn't worth the fights that ensued when I moved any of his piles, which he referred to as his "filing system." I eked out a two-inch crevice between the computer and the printer that allowed me to prop up a few folders. It took three years to have the sense to get my own lap top so I could have the flexibility to work on any surface in the house.

Over the next few months, we played an uneasy game of adjusting. Larry spent a great deal of time following me around closing cabinet doors and drawers I continually left open, a bad habit I had had my entire life. I learned to accept the fact that he was king of the television remote. He could watch several television shows simultaneously, including a couple of basketball games, reruns of *The Big Bang Theory*, and a showing of a favorite movie. I found this tolerable as long as I was multi-tasking on the couch—doing a crossword puzzle, checking emails, reading a book, and cutting coupons—while he ruled the remote. My annoying habit cancelled out his.

I am not the only person who has experienced post-retirement angst. One friend, whose son had been in a playgroup with our son over thirty years earlier, told me that her husband had acquired this overwhelming need to be with her wherever she went. Grocery shopping, dropping off mail at the post office, running to the drug store for a prescription, was now regarded by Steve as a two-person outing. "If Larry isn't busy," Fern suggested, "maybe we can arrange a weekly playdate between our two husbands. Then I can get out of the house by myself for a couple of hours."

My friend Judy commented that only after they were both retired did she realize how 'uber-organized' her husband was. A week before they left for their two-month stay in Florida, Judy was haphazardly stacking clothing on her bed and throwing cosmetics and toiletries into a bin. Charlie strolled into the bedroom and opened up his file marked "Florida." It included a detailed list of everything he needed to pack, including the number of pairs of socks, shirts, and shoes he was bringing. Another list included restaurants in Naples, with notes on ratings and menus. He even planned their drive down to Florida in minute detail: He had researched hotels and restaurants en route on Trip Advisor, printed out weather forecasts from *weather.com,* and created a chart of estimated travel times between stops from Google maps. "He researches every single detail and isn't willing to leave anything to chance," Judy said. "It's driving me nuts!"

Quite a few of my friends have commented that their retired husbands, who managed people all their working life, feel the need to manage their wives. "Marty loves to come up with projects," Melanie shared with me over coffee. "He suggests these projects on a weekly basis, pointing out, for example, that the linen closet needs to be reorganized or the bookshelves in the fourth bedroom need to be cleaned out. Of course, Marty is the idea person. I am the person who is expected to *implement* his projects."

When I talk to couples about adjusting to retirement, I find that the wives are much more forthcoming about their experiences. The men I spoke to, for the most part, were oblivious.

This is not just part of our generation. Joanne, a friend from North Dakota, remembered mediating a fight between her in-laws. After many years of farming acres of wheat and soy, the husband had decided to help his wife with her vegetable garden. While they were cutting up potatoes for planting, he insisted that each potato mound have five eyes. The wife explained that she had always limited the mounds to three eyes. When he tried to drag his daughter-in-law into the discussion, Joanne demurred, saying, "I am sure it all depends on the year." Joanne said, in the end, they decided on four eyes, a nice compromise.

Compromise—the bottom line as two people learn to live their dream, to spend most of their time together. Maybe love is relearning give-and-take and embracing each other's quirks.

My favorite piece of advice came from a man who held a high position in the federal government for many years before he and his wife retired. "I get to make the big decisions," he explained. "Who should run for president of the United States. Whether or not we should go to war with Syria. And she makes the less important decisions, such as where we live, what we eat, with whom we spend our time, when and where we are going on vacation. It works out really well for us." As I hope it works out for all the retired love birds I know and love.

TWENTY TWO

Bluebird Powder Day

While visiting my daughter and son-in-law in Frisco, Colorado, I went cross country skiing for the first time in several years. It seemed like everything was in place. Clothes? Check. Skis and poles? Check, Beautiful snow cover? Check. Perfect temperature? Check. Ability to cross country ski? Not so good!

Julie had moved to Colorado after college for a "one year" teaching position at a science school near Vail. She fell in love with the mountains, the snow—and Sam. They were married in Moab, Utah, in May 2007. After completing master's degrees and finding permanent jobs, they purchased a home in Frisco, a small town 9100 feet above sea level on the western slope of the Continental Divide.

Larry and I visited Julie and Sam at least once a year, usually around the Fourth of July. We arrived in time for the parade, the town celebration, Julie and Sam's annual BBQ, and the fireworks over Lake Dillon. Julie and Sam had fully embraced the Colorado winter life style and had encouraged us to visit them during the snow season. For many years, we demurred because of our work schedule. After we retired, Larry and I preferred to spend our winter months getting away from snow and cold, NOT heading in the opposite direction to *more* snow and *more* cold. In 2014, as I missed my daughter, I made the decision that I would go to the mountains in the winter, even if Larry wouldn't join me.

As soon as I entered the kitchen my first morning there, Julie asked me if I wanted to cross country ski. She and Sam live only a couple of blocks from the Frisco recreation/bike trail, and the snow was fresh enough for us to ski right from their house. I agreed to give it a try.

Julie fit me with a set of boots, poles, and skis. I snapped my right foot into the right ski easily, but the left boot/left ski didn't cooperate. Six to eight tries later, both of my skis were snapped in. By the time we finished, the bottom of Julie's skis were stuck with snow. She took them off, went back into the house to locate the scraper, chipped the snow off her skis, and put them back on. Then she showed me how to lift up each ski at a ninety degree angle and balance on the other leg while she removed the snow and ice from the bottom of my skis. Once we were done, we headed out of the driveway towards the bike path.

The snow was as beautiful as anticipated. I naively thought that cross country skiing would be like riding a bike: Once my skis were on, I would be gliding along the path like a pro. However, I was a little older, a little less flexible, and a little heavier. My progress was pathetic. Fortunately, Julie was a good teacher. She reviewed with me how to kick up my heels, how to glide, how to lean forward to get better momentum. But despite my attempts, I always was at least two hundred yards behind her.

Twenty minutes later, I was bathed in sweat, breathing heavily to compensate for the altitude, and seriously questioning my ability to ski another yard. I didn't want to disappoint Julie. I soldiered along.

We poked along for a mile or so, and Julie suggested we scrape off the sticking snow from the bottom of my ski as we practiced at home. I kicked out my left ski, tried balancing on my right leg, and crashed to the ground. After several attempts to get up, I finally had to remove my skis to right myself. Now I had to get back into the bindings. Multiple unsuccessful tries later, Julie initial patience was wearing thin. She pointed impatiently to the spot on the binder where the boot snapped in. "Right here?" I asked.

"Yes!" she answered. I put my toe in and snapped the binding down—on my poor daughter's finger. She spewed out a string of obscenities fit for an angry, drunken sailor.

"I'm so sorry!" I exclaimed. "But where did you learn that language?"

After a couple of more tries, I was into my bindings and on our way again. We had to stop a couple of more times to scrape our skis, but I was enjoying the experience.

Forty-five minutes later, we were home, cozy, warm, and enjoying a cup of hot tea.

Sam came down from the home office where he had been working. "You're back! How did it go?" he asked.

"I'm a little rusty," I said, "but I'm catching on."

"How far did you go?" he asked.

"Actual miles were around three," I said. "For Julie it must have felt like to *hell* and back."

The next morning, I woke up feeling pain in muscles I didn't remember I had. But when I went down to breakfast, Julie was ready to try it again. A half an hour later, we were back on the bike path. My skis clipped in on the first try, and the wax helped me glide smoothly over the fresh tracks Julie broke in front of me. I could not stop smiling. When I fell down, I picked myself up with no difficulty.

"You're doing so much better this morning, Mom," commented Julie. "Are you enjoying yourself?"

"Every minute!" I responded.

"This is a bluebird powder day," Julie said.

"What does that mean?" I asked.

"It's a Colorado expression," explained Julie. "The sun is shining, the sky is a brilliant blue, the snow is a perfect powder, and the temperature is ideal."

"You're right, Julie," I said. "It *is* a bluebird powder day!" And we continued gliding through the white snow.

TWENTY THREE

Never Mind the Bucket List! Just Live It!

One winter afternoon while living in the Capital District, Larry and I had lunch at a Chinese restaurant with a former co-worker of his who was planning on retiring in a few more months.

"Can you two give me some guidelines as to what I should do when I leave the job?" she asked. She knew that she had to do *something*. She couldn't picture herself just sitting home and having no structure to her life. "I certainly don't want to be bored!" she explained.

Four years earlier, Larry and I were both in our last months of work after long careers in public service and education. People were continually asking us what *we* were going to do after we retired. Larry had a simple, straightforward plan: We would travel, and we spend more time volunteering for Special Olympics.

I, however, fearing boredom, felt the need to line up more ducks to keep me happy. What would I do with my life once I did not fill my time with a forty plus hour a week job? I too sought advice from friends and relatives who had retired before me on how I could survive all the "free time."

"What free time?" commented a former superintendent of schools, who has spent his retirement volunteering on numerous boards and organizations. "If you want to be in control of your time, keep on working."

"You'll never look back," a former co-worker stated. "You will wonder how you ever worked as your days will be so full."

I wasn't convinced.

Larry retired in May 2010, but I still headed to the office for seven more months. I left the house at 7:30 each morning after kissing my sleeping husband's head as he nestled under the covers. He made up for it by having dinner ready for me when I arrived home. However, my desire to join him pushed me into a pre-retirement blitz at work. I confirmed my retirement date with my boss, went to a New York State Education Teacher's Retirement System seminar to line up the paperwork, and began cleaning out my files. Then I turned my attention to creating and implementing my retirement bucket list.

First on the list were all those hobbies that had been put on the back burner. The short list, in addition to travel and Special Olympics, included the following:

1. Read all the books on my "Read Before I Die" list;
2. Complete the crewel piece I started twenty years earlier;
3. Learn how to knit;
4. Update my fifty photo albums;
5. Organize the two drawers in my file cabinet filled with my children's artwork, report cards, and special projects;
6. Relearn French;
7. Learn Spanish;
8. Put together all of my stories and my mother's stories into a book.

Yes, this woman was going to be productive in her golden years!

Although I already had a number of unread books on my book shelves, I hit a couple of used book sales and downloaded numerous classics onto my Nook. I purchased orange and royal blue yarn and needles to knit Larry a Syracuse University scarf. On impulse I also bought Red Sox theme flannel to make him a throw to commemorate his favorite baseball team.

At the office supply store, I selected new photo albums to replace the ones that were falling apart as well as file folders, labels, and markers for my home organization project. I downloaded a language app for my *français redux* and purchased a *Spanish for Dummies* for my *español*. Mom's files were piled six inches thick into a drawer, ready to polish and publish.

Throughout this entire process, Larry looked on with a mix of mild amusement to outright incredulity that I needed to prepare so much. And he feared all these projects and books and anticipated classes were going to fill my dance card so much we won't have time to just *be*.

After all the planning and anticipation, my last day of work arrived. On December 17, 2010, I fought the traffic on the Northway and Route 7 one last time. I completed the required written instructions to my successor, signed my exiting papers, and said my final goodbyes. Then I drove my last rush hour trip home to Clifton Park. It was time to tackle that bucket list!

I reflected on all this planning over the dinner with Larry's co-worker. I thought of the hundreds of unread books on my shelves that had been passed over for more current ones in the local library. An added bonus: I could get them in big print, a big advantage for my "golden years" eyes.

I tried to work on the Elsa Williams crewel piece. My eyes had changed since I started it, and I doubted it would ever be finished.

The knitting? Abandoned after four unsuccessful attempts at learning how to cast on. The Red Sox throw? I pinned it together, but I never took out the sewing machine to stitch up the sides.

The pictures were still in envelopes, the photo albums still unwrapped. This was 2014, the digital age, and I needed to think of tossing most of them, scanning the favorites, and putting them into a digital album. My children strongly encouraged me to toss—not organize—all the childhood memorabilia I had saved. I haven't had time to refresh my French or learn Spanish; I needed time to work on my own English as I edited and re-edited my stories and my mother's story for *The Jewish World*. At least I was working on one of those items on my bucket list.

So what did we do those first four years since we retired? We traveled to Machu Picchu, the Galápagos Islands, the Danube, Bryce and Zion. When we were home, we spent time volunteering for Special Olympics—coaching track and field and bowling. Yes, in the end, Larry's simple, straightforward approach to retirement was the most realistic.

Most importantly, the most satisfying activities of the retirement years in Clifton Park were in many cases activities that were never on my radar. Weekly visits to a couple of friends at Daughters of Sarah nursing home evolved into my volunteering at their memory enhancement unit. After taking Zumba at a local elementary school, I realized how much I loved exercise classes and joined the YMCA.

Over dim sum on that cold winter afternoon, Larry and I offered this advice to our friend: Yes, you can speculate as to what you would like to do once you leave your job for the last time. However, you may never get to many of them. As a matter of fact, you should just kick the bucket—the bucket list that is. Let life take you where you had only dreamed of going. And that is actually the best retirement advice of all.

TWENTY FOUR

Manna from Heaven: Vanilla Ice Cream

My maiden name is Cohen. In all honesty, however, it should have been *Cone*. As in ice cream cone. As in my favorite summertime/anytime treat. As a matter of fact, if I were one of the Israelis wandering the desert with Moses, my manna from heaven would have tasted like Breyer's Natural Vanilla.

My love for ice cream is in my genetic makeup. While I was growing up, a day wasn't complete in the Cohen household without our dishes of ice cream. In the 1950s in our small town, choices were limited. Our freezer usually held one or two half gallons of Sealtest Neapolitan. Having all three flavors for six people worked out well. My father chose vanilla topped with a huge helping of strawberry preserves. My mother went for the strawberry. The four children took whatever we could scoop up with our vintage gray aluminum Scoop Rite ice cream scoop.

Our favorite food also played into all of our family's special occasions. We dished out ice cream at birthday celebrations, Yom Kippur break-the-fasts, the first post-Passover meal, and Thanksgiving—what was apple pie without the *à la mode*! As an added treat, my parents would take us for ice cream at the Frosty Dairy Bar, a restaurant on Route 9 in Plattsburgh. Going there allowed us to go beyond Neapolitan, giving me my first tastes of "exotic" flavors like pistachio, chocolate chip, and cherry vanilla.

Fortunately, I met and married a man who, although not as fanatical as me, enjoys ice cream. He loves me enough to tolerate my addiction. Otherwise, I doubt if the marriage would have lasted. Our first date was a movie and a trip to Friendly's. Larry had a chocolate Fribble, and I had a hot fudge sundae with—you guessed it—vanilla ice cream. It became our go-to place after every movie or play for many years.

Once we had children, we usually kept at least one half gallon of ice cream in the freezer, vanilla for me and Stewart's Swiss chocolate almond for Larry—he still hasn't forgiven Stewart's for phasing out his favorite flavor. Once they could hold a kiddie cone, we would bring Adam and Julie during summer months to the Country Drive-In, a popular hamburger/soft-serve ice cream stand off Exit 8 of the Northway. Julie took Larry there on Father's Day for a hamburger, fries, and an ice cream cone during her junior high years.

My now-adult children don't place ice cream as high on their favorite food list, but they take care of their mother. Julie and Sam make sure they have Haagen-Dazs ice cream or gelato waiting for us in their freezer when we visit them Colorado. Adam treats us to Bi-Rite Creamery ice cream in a waffle cone whenever we visit him in San Francisco.

As empty nesters, we usually have a half gallon of vanilla ice cream in the freezer. I will have a small scoop once a week. Larry will indulge a little more often using his own "in-house ice cream routine." First he softens the ice cream by putting the whole carton into the microwave for a few seconds. He then uses the Scoop Rite ice cream scoop we inherited from my parents to transfer one or two scoops into a cereal bowl. He squirts on Hershey's Special Dark chocolate syrup, throws on a few Ghirardelli dark chocolate chips, and tosses on a healthy handful of chopped walnuts and sliced almonds. When Larry was laid up with a leg surgery, I tried to cheer him up by 'recreating' his masterpiece. I failed miserably as I messed up the proportions of ice cream, chocolate syrup, and nuts. To be honest, I think Larry treats ice cream as another way to eat nuts. For me, however, a simple unadorned dish or cone of vanilla ice cream is my favorite food, a link to my childhood as well as one of life's great pleasures.

Ice cream even has played an important role during one of the most poignant times of my life. When my mother fell gravely ill four days before she passed away, she lost her desire for food. I asked her if she wanted anything special to eat. She whispered, "Strawberry ice cream." The cafe at Coburg Village, the independent living place where she was living, had none. The young woman working behind the counter, upon hearing the story, went up to the main restaurant and brought me back a huge dish of strawberry ice cream to honor my mother's request. When I got back to Mom's bedside, she ate three or four spoonfuls before she pushed my hand away. "That was delicious! Thank you!" That was the last food she ever ate, a true Cohen to the end. I can only hope that I, like my mother, will have a long, happy, healthy life that concludes with the sweet taste of vanilla ice cream on my tongue.

Until we relocated to Florida, one of my favorite stops was the three-mile trip to the Country Drive-In for a vanilla soft serve. As a matter of fact, I needed to make a trip there to take a picture of my eating ice cream for *The Jewish World*. It was a cold, rainy, day, making it quite tough for me to purchase the cone and eat it. Someone had to do the job, however, and who better than Marilyn *Cone* Shapiro?

TWENTY FIVE
I Would Do It All Again:
Dealing with Aging Parents

When my parents moved up from Florida to Coburg Village in 2005, we knew they were settling into a place that offered them independence and the kind of life they wanted to lead. As it was only four miles from our home, Larry and I, as well as my siblings, had peace of mind knowing we were close enough to be there when they needed us and to watch over their physical and emotional health. At times, however, providing that oversight was not easy.

Every Sunday, Larry and I had a standing date with my parents to go out to eat at a local restaurant. Mom's favorite choice was a Chinese buffet as she loved spare ribs and anything fried. Dad said he preferred Italian, although his choices in those restaurants were sometimes more McDonalds than *mangiare bene.* He once insisted on our driving to an Italian restaurant in Schenectady in the dead of winter and proceeded to order minestrone soup and chicken nuggets.

One week, on the advice of friends, we decided to take them to Verdile's, a landmark Italian restaurant in Troy. As was the custom, Larry and I picked them up in the front of their building. I helped my father get into the front passenger seat, helped my mother get into the back seat behind Dad, and took my place behind Larry. Larry put the car in gear and headed to our destination. Around two miles down the road, my father said, "Oh, damn! I forgot my teeth!"

"We'll turn around and get them," offered Larry.

"That's okay," said Dad. "I can just gum my food."

Larry ignored him and turned the car around.

When we got back to Coburg, I took my parents' keys, went through the foyer, ran up the stairs to their second floor apartment, unlocked the door, grabbed a set of dentures out of a bowl in the bathroom, wrapped them in a paper towel, relocked the door, and headed back to the car.

"Thanks, Marilyn," said Dad, as he started putting them into his mouth. A second later, he yelled, "Hey! These aren't my teeth!"

"Oh, they must be mine!" Mom chimed in from the back seat. "I forgot them too! Hand them back, Bill!"

As Mom was getting her bridge into her mouth, I went back to the apartment, found the second bowl with the *Dad's* teeth on the bathroom vanity, and ran back to the car. Now that all the dentures were in place, we were ready to complete our trip to Verdile's.

All was fairly quiet for a couple of miles. "I read an interesting article in *Consumer Reports* this week about one of my prescription medicines," Dad piped up. "You know how I am always having to run to the bathroom? Well, that's one of the side effects of one of the damn pills I have to take."

"You have congestive heart failure, Dad," I said. "Your doctor put you on diuretics to prevent fluid from building up in your lungs. You've landed in the Ellis Hospital emergency room three times since you moved here when you failed to take them."

"Well, the heck with all these doctors!" said Dad. "I am tired of constantly having to pee. I've decided to stop taking them. Haven't swallowed of those suckers for four days!"

I immediately conjured up in my mind another ambulance ride for Dad and another lost day of work for me. Meanwhile, I thought Larry was going to drive off the road.

Mom patted my hand and whispered to me, "I'll take care of this, sweetheart. Don't worry." By the time we got to the restaurant, all four of us were on edge, hungry, and ready for a good dinner. Fortunately, Verdile's lived up to its reputation. Our pasta-based meals were delicious, and the staff was friendly, kind and accommodating. Judging from the demographics of the people sitting around the room, the staff in the restaurant was obviously used to serving senior citizens.

As our waiter cleared the table before he brought coffee, my mother popped out her bridge and wrapped it in a napkin. Although I was used to this in our own homes, I was a little grossed out that she was doing it in public. I also worried she'd lose them—an expensive proposition.

I started to stammer an explanation and warning to the waiter. "Err…please don't take the napkin. My mother's teeth are in it."

He broke out in a big smile. "Don't worry! We're used to that here. Can't tell you how many times we've had to do a dumpster dive for a set of false teeth or a hearing aid!"

We drank our coffee, paid the bill, and drove my parents back to Coburg Village. The next day, I called my mother, and she assured me that Dad was back on his water pills.

"Thanks for dinner, Marilyn," Mom said. "Dad and I really enjoyed our afternoon with the two of you. We'll have to come up with another fun place to eat next Sunday."

"Sure, Mom," I said aloud. "Let's do that!" In my mind, however, I was thinking, 'Let's just make it less exciting.'

The four of us enjoyed many more Sunday outings until my father's passing in November 2008. Larry and I kept up the tradition with my mother until her death in March 2011. To this day, despite the misplaced teeth, the medical revelations, and the not-so-healthy Chinese buffets, we fondly remember those Sunday dinners we shared with Mom and Dad.

TWENTY SIX

Wrong Way Shapiro Travels the World

Larry and I met at a Purim party forty-three years ago. He was King Ahasuerus to my Queen Esther. All in all, it has been a successful match and a successful marriage. However, Larry has told me that if he realized how directionally impaired I was when he first met me, he is not sure if he would have pursued the relationship. In other words, if his Queen Esther had had to find her way to the palace, King Ahasuerus still would have been married to Vashti.

Larry is one of those people who is endowed with the ability not only to follow directions perfectly but also to intuitively know what direction he should go when lost. I don't know if he is part bloodhound, but he knows when to turn right, left, or whatever and get us where we are supposed to go.

I, on the other hand, can get lost going through a revolving door. It doesn't matter where I am going. I need specific, detailed instructions, including street names, recognizable landmarks—the Walgreens on the corner; the elementary school on the right; a Target store on the left—and exact mileage between all of them. And I would *still* screw up.

You would think things would improve with the invention of the GPS. Initially even that failed me, as demonstrated by my first attempt to use one to navigate my way to a business breakfast south of Albany.

The machine kept rejecting the address I typed in, so I simplified the address to just the name of the road. The directions down the expressways were excellent. When I turned on to River Road, however, an annoying female voice—whom I already named Mappie—chirped, "You have arrived at your destination." I yelled at her, "No, Mappie! I am not there yet! You need to get me to the building"

I was now lost and encountering another problem. If there was a speed limit posted on River Road, I couldn't find it. I didn't know if it was 30 or 55 miles per hour. I erred on the side of safety and kept my speed to around 30. A couple of cars got on my tail and passed me, and I just kept looking for the building.

Suddenly, I saw a policeman's flashing lights behind me. I pulled over, rolled down my window, and asked the policeman if I was speeding. He said, "No ma'am, you were going too slow. You are a road hazard."

"I am so sorry, sir, but it's not my fault," I explained. "It's the stupid GPS! Mappie told me that I arrived at my destination, but she was wrong!" Thankfully, the officer took pity on me. "Look, lady, the building you are looking for is a mile down the road on the left," he said. "I'm not going to give you a ticket this time, but next time, print out the directions from MapQuest before you get into your car."

Fortunately, Larry the Scout has been the designated driver for most of our married life. He was perfectly happy to drive while I would sit in the passenger seat, either reading a book or sleeping. After we retired, Larry and I started taking longer car trips, and Larry decided to give me more responsibility. On the way to Arches National Park, Larry insisted that I take out the map he had gotten from AAA and keep track of the routes. Wrong Way Shapiro, who actually got lost going to my own apartment, found map reading a joy. Not only would I follow the map, but I also would plug in the GPS and accompany the two with one or two guidebooks. I kept Larry up-to-date on our location as well as geographic trivia. "We're heading into

Fruita, Colorado," I reported. "Population is 12,724; elevation 4511 feet. Town is famous for Mike the Headless Chicken."

I have unfortunately been known to rely too heavily on the route suggested by Google Maps without considering alternative routes. On a trip to Florida, Larry and I were driving up the West Coast from Sarasota to Dunedin. Google map took us directly through the heart of Tampa and its gridlock. Larry insisted that he had told me that we were to take a route that ran ABOVE Tampa. I either never heard him or his memory was wrong. The argument in our car could be heard all the way back to Sarasota.

Larry decided the only way to avoid future arguments based on the best route was to call up the directions on MapQuest before we headed out. I would then trace them on a map. We used this combination on one of our last visits in Florida from the East Coast to Naples. We successfully navigated our way from Vero Beach, over the top of Lake Okeechobee (even finding a quicker route on the map not suggested by MapQuest), and down I-75 to Naples. We made our left hand turn off the I-75 ramp, drove confidently into the targeted community, and pulled triumphantly into the driveway. Unfortunately, the wrong driveway. I had gotten the street name correct, but had written down the wrong house number.

Oh well. At least I didn't have to act as the navigator for our plane back to Albany.

TWENTY SEVEN

Go Jump in the Lake! Freezin' For a Reason

I had always been intrigued by news articles and pictures of polar plunges, where hundreds of smiling people clad in only bathing suits dive into a body of water in the middle of the winter. Participants say they are having fun. I never understood their enthusiasm until I found myself diving into Lake George—water temperature around 50 degrees—on a brisk November day. Crazy? Yes! Glad I did it? Double yes. Because I was freezin' for a reason. I was raising money for Special Olympics Capital Region.

Special Olympics is the world's largest sports organization for children and adults with intellectual disabilities. The Special Olympics New York Capital Region provides year-round training and competitions to more than sixteen hundred athletes from twelve counties in fourteen different sports. For a number of years, Larry and I were involved as Saratoga County Special Olympics track and field and bowling coaches.

We also participated in Special Olympic fundraisers. One of the most popular and well known in the Capital District is the Polar Plunge, where hundreds of people plunge into Lake George on the third Saturday of November.

In a moment of insanity, I had signed up and participated in the plunge in 2011. Larry had a list of reasons why it was *not going* to be a joint effort: He needed to be on the shore to hold my bathrobe and towel. He needed to take pictures. He needed to drive me home as I would be too cold to handle the wheel. He didn't want to take the spotlight away from "my" event. Maybe he had more common sense than the rest of us, or maybe he just didn't know how to have fun. Within minutes of coming out of the water that first time, however, I swore to anyone with ear shot that I would never do it again. Our schedule in 2012 prevented a repeat plunge, and I was thinking of finding another excuse for 2013 until...

In a second moment of insanity, I committed to participate in the 2013 event. I rejoined Freezin' Friends, a team of plungers headed by Joni Rhodes, whose son Nick participated in several Special Olympic events, including our track and field program. It was time for me to again raise money to support athletes like Nick

In the middle of September, I began a fundraising blitz, mostly through emails and Facebook. The response was overwhelming. I had pledges from family and friends across the country and even from England. Most pledged on line, but many others handed me checks or cash, commenting "Better you than me!" and "Boy, you are brave!" By the day of the plunge, our team had raised close to $5000, and the region total was approaching $77,000.

By this time, you would think that I would be mentally and physically ready to dive back into Lake George. I hadn't died the first time; my heart had held out; I hadn't even caught a cold. But in the days leading up to the plunge, I had nightmares about going into a freezing lake. In addition, this year I was going to top what I had started in 2011. In my first year, most of my supporters congratulated me and praised my bravery for plunging up to my neck. However, a few people kiddingly questioned as if I had ever gone in the lake, as my hair was still dry, and the water droplets on my body didn't show well on the photos. This time, I was going to make sure that pictures showed a soaked bathing suit and a wet head so that no one would doubt my commitment.

We were fortunate with the weather. The morning of the plunge was a sunny, calm day, with air temperatures in the fifties. Larry and I stopped at the registration desk and then headed down to Shepard's Park Beach. Over my bathing suit, I had flannel pants, a thermal shirt, my Polar Plunge sweatshirt, and a warm terry bathrobe. Under my water shoes were heavy woolen socks. I found Joni in her traditional Dr. Seuss hat she had worn for each of the seven plunges in which she previously participated. I recognized most of my teammates from 2011, a mix of Nick's family, friends, and Special Olympics coaches. In addition, a large group of students from Schuylerville High School had signed up for the fundraiser to support Nick, their classmate. Joni provided all thirty members of the team with a choice of colors in Santa hats.

Several other teams of plungers were also on the beach, including Max's Buddies, Freeze Duchenne, Brian's Bashers, and members of the Siena men's baseball team. We spent the next couple of hours munching on bagels, sipping hot coffee, taking pictures, and connecting with members of our team and the other plungers. Several were in costume: capes, polar bear hats, boas, and, in the case of one man, a skimpy beige bikini bathing suit. "My Miley Cyrus look," he explained.

At ten minutes before noon, all the plungers stripped down to their bathing suits. Shivering despite the warm sun, we lined up to wait for the signal to hit the water. At exactly twelve noon, led by three athletes holding the Special Olympics torch, over five hundred and fifty crazies—including me—streamed into Lake George.

As my ankles hit the water, I faced my first obstacle. As our team was near the end of the line, we were going into the lake when the members of the Siena men's baseball team were coming out. Fast. Blindly, with no concern for who was in their way. I darted through hurling bodies until I found a clear spot in the water, took a deep breath, and dove in, orange Santa hat and all.

OH MY G-D! Why didn't I remember it was this cold! I immediately thought of those poor people on the Titanic. I had visions of Leonardo DiCaprio's Jack clinging onto the edge of the makeshift raft that held Kate Winslet's Rose. I could not get out of the water fast enough. I ran onto the sand, hair and body dripping, searching desperately for Larry and, more importantly, my bathrobe and towel. As soon as I found him, I asked, "Did you get a picture?" Larry said yes, but I must have had ice in my ears. I didn't hear him and headed back into the water for a second totally unnecessary photo opportunity.

I have to say that the second plunge that day wasn't as bad as the first time. Maybe the sun had warmed my body. Or I was so numb I couldn't tell the difference. Larry took a couple of more pictures, and I was finally able to head for the women's warming tent, where I quickly changed into dry clothes. We drove back to Clifton Park with the car's heater going full blast.

Later that afternoon, Larry and I talked about the plunge over large bowls of steaming chicken and rice noodle soup at a local Chinese restaurant. "Next year, I need to wear a different bathing suit and a pair of shorts as those pictures I posted on Facebook are just too embarrassing," I said. "And maybe if I start fundraising earlier, I can raise more money."

Larry nodded, "Let's just see what happens with our schedule next year."

I was not able to plunge in 2014, and by 2015, we had moved to Florida. Joni emailed me the first fall we were the South to ask kiddingly if I would like to come up to Lake George to participate, but I declined. So far, I haven't joined any polar plunges in Florida. Maybe an alligator wrestling fundraising event? We'll have to wait and see.

TWENTY EIGHT

Advice for the New Parent: You Know What's Best!

When our daughter Julie was expecting our first grandchild, she called me to tell me about the children of her friends, both around eighteen months old. She commented that the little boy is a little fussy and needy, with frequent meltdowns. Her other friend's child is easy, calm and sweet; her name, "Grace," says it all. Julie said that she hopes her child is like Grace. My comment? "So you want a Grace, not a Julie, huh?" Not surprisingly, she wasn't appreciative of my observation.

Larry and I were ecstatic at the prospect of becoming grandparents. Julie and Sam had been married eight years prior to her pregnancy, and I wasn't sure if they wanted to have children. Over Thanksgiving, 2014, however, on a walk along the Mohawk River bike path, we learned they were expecting a baby. Sam pointedly asked me how we were enjoying our hot tub. I told him how much we loved going in on cold November days, "A day like today!" I offered them towels, robes, a bottle of wine, and privacy.

"I can't go into the hot tub, Mom," piped up Julie. "And I can't have a glass of wine."

"Why not?" I asked.

"Because [—pregnant pause—] I am carrying your grandchild."

Once I stopped jumping up and down, and once we promised we would not share the news with ANYONE until at least mid-January, I began reflecting on words of advice I could give to the new parents. On Mother's Day 2015, in honor of her impending motherhood, I gave Julie the following advice:

Nothing will prepare you for the moment you hold your baby for the first time. Throughout my first pregnancy, Larry and I were thrilled about becoming parents. However, Larry and I had several discussions as to how our life would not change that drastically once s/he was born. We would bring our child everywhere. We would continue to travel and work and socialize as we had done before. Once we each had held Adam in our arms for less than a minute, however, we knew that our lives were never going to be the same. The reality of taking care of a tiny, dependent being who needed every ounce of our physical and emotional attention to survive put any ideas of "business as usual" out the window. In fact, we didn't mind turning our lives upside down. We would move mountains to make sure our son was well fed, dry, content, and especially safe. Three years later, I harbored similar thoughts regarding status quo while awaiting the birth of our second child. During my pregnancy, I thought to myself, "Okay baby, I will love you, but just know that we already have a child, and he will come first." Again, I was proven wrong. The bonding was immediate and powerful, and our arms and hearts were more than big enough to accommodate another child.

Children don't grow like lettuce. Whenever I encountered a bump in the road while raising our children, whether it was braces or a bad track meet or a broken heart, my mother would offer her favorite expression. Unlike lettuce, she would remind me, which you just put in the ground as a bunch of seeds and harvest thirty days later, children are work intensive. Things don't always go smoothly, and you don't sail through the eighteen years until they head off for college. It took me a while to realize raising children was more like growing prized orchids. And I have no green thumb.

"Give your child roots to grow and wings to fly." The Dalai Lama. While raising these "delicate orchids," Larry and I tried provide Adam and Julie with a supportive nurturing environment throughout their formative years. We tried to give them moral values, a strong sense of community and personal responsibility. It was not until Julie packed up her life in my used Toyota and moved to Colorado, and Adam headed to the West Coast for law school and life in San Francisco, that the second part of Dalai Lama's words wholeheartedly hit me. Oh, how I envy my friends who have children ten minutes away! I would even settle for three hundred miles. But this was not to be. They have forged a life a long plane ride—or two!—away. They both have put down their own roots far from where we live but are happy, settled, content, and doing what they need to do. We hope the root system we gave them will guide their wings on their journeys.

You ultimately know what is best for your child. When Adam was six weeks old, I drove him to a local mall for our first shopping trip since he was born. I put him in a red umbrella stroller and pushed him through the stores. A woman stopped me and said, "Oh my goodness! Your baby is all crunched up in that stroller, pale as a ghost! He looks dead!" I immediately pulled Adam out from carriage. He began howling with rage because I had jarred him awake. As she walked away, the "baby expert" commented, "Oh! I guess he was okay!" I learned quickly that I knew what I was doing, not some stranger. Remember those roots your parents gave you? Trust that they will help you grow as a parent.

Ironically, during Julie's pregnancy, friends gave *us* advice about grand-parenting. We were told repeatedly that the moment we held our granddaughter in our arms for the first time, our life would never be the same. "It's different with a grandchild," a friend said. "It is as if you are holding your future." We even got advice about when, where, and how to give advice to Julie and Sam. Until then, I hoped that the "momilies" I gave Julie that Mother's Day would be taken in the spirit in which they are given—with much joy and love.

TWENTY NINE

Chasing the Elusive Georgia O'Keeffe

In January 2016, Larry and I attended a lecture on Georgia O'Keeffe, part of an artist series offered in our Florida community. It was a relief to drive only three miles to the lecture. You see, we have been chasing Georgia across the country for years.

Growing up in Keeseville, New York, I had little opportunity to visit museums and galleries, much less to develop art appreciation. In college, I avoided "killer" Art History 101 as I was too obsessed with my grade point average to venture out too far beyond my literature and education courses.

Larry took some art courses at Northeastern University and spent time in Boston museums. One of our first dates was a trip to the Sterling Clark Museum in Williamstown, Massachusetts. Our interest in art grew along with our marriage. Fall leaf peeping trips included the Norman Rockwell and Grandma Moses museums. In New York City, we explored the Metropolitan, the Guggenheim, and the Museum of Modern Art. As our travels expanded, we visited museums in San Francisco, Lima, and London. We knew what we liked: We walked quickly past Renaissance art with its stiff and tortured religious images and headed for the Impressionists—Monet, Manet, Degas.

Although we had seen and appreciated Georgia O'Keeffe's work when we viewed her occasional pieces in major cities, our interest was heightened as a result of a college visit. One of our nephews was accepted to St. Johns' College in Santa Fe, New Mexico. Larry offered to fly out with him to see the school and explore the area. When they returned, Larry could not stop talking about the Georgia O'Keeffe Museum and its collection of her paintings. He loved the colors and the creativity. He promised that we would travel to Santa Fe together so he could share his find with me.

Less than a year later, we made plans to visit Santa Fe as part of our annual summer visit with Julie and Sam in Colorado. We researched lodging, restaurants, the art district, the historic downtown. On top of the list was the O'Keeffe Museum and Ghost Ranch, O'Keeffe's New Mexico residence for many years.

Fate intervened from the start. A series of wildfires had hit New Mexico. As we traveled south on the highway, an ominous cloud of smoke loomed above us. At one point, we considered completely abandoning our plans and going back to Colorado. As we learned more about the situation, we scaled down our expectations. We would skip Ghost Ranch, which was closer to the fires, and limit our visit to just the historic city.

Our destination on our first full day in Santa Fe was the O'Keeffe museum. As we walked the short distance from our bed and breakfast, Larry chatted about diverse subjects that O'Keeffe painted—the New York cityscapes, the flowers, the Northern New Mexican landscapes. When we got there, however, we saw a huge sign announcing that the majority of O'Keeffe paintings were on tour in Europe. Instead, the museum was proud to present an exhibit of Norman Rockwell sketches and paintings. We could not believe that we had traveled so far to see O'Keeffe only to view drawings by the popular New England artist. Yes, we liked Rockwell and his iconic *Saturday Evening Post* covers. But we experienced his work every fall as part of our annual leaf peeping tour of New England. We had to drive less than one hour across the New York border to go to the Rockwell Museum in

Stockbridge, Massachusetts. Needless to say, I was disappointed.

We soon had another chance. In 2014, the Hyde Museum in Glens Falls, less than an hour north of us, was sponsoring a special exhibit entitled "Modern Nature: Georgia O'Keeffe and Lake George." The family of O'Keeffe's husband Albert Stieglitz owned a place in Lake George, and O'Keeffe had spent summers there during their marriage. We knew we weren't going to be seeing many flowers, but seeing her interpretations of Lake George would be interesting.

The exhibit opened in the summer. Friends reported back to us that lines were long and the place was jammed. We decided to postpone our visit until after Labor Day when the crowds thinned. Stymied again! Larry tore his Achilles tendon. He underwent surgery and sported a bulky cast on his leg for eight weeks. By the time Larry felt up to going, the exhibit was long gone.

The following February, Larry and I flew out to San Francisco to visit our son Adam. On the plane, we met a couple from the Capital Region. She had been involved in art and served as a docent for the Hyde Museum. We shared with her our sad saga of thwarted attempts to see the O'Keeffe exhibit. "Did you know the DeYoung Museum in San Francisco currently is running the same exhibit?" she asked. No, we didn't know. As soon as we arrived in Adam's apartment, we suggested to him that we go to the DeYoung together. It was a surprisingly short walk from his apartment to the museum, and we actually got to see the exhibit. We lingered over the paintings and portraits and even listened to a lecture. Our chase was over.

Larry and I enjoyed the lecture down in Florida. Forty minutes into her talk, however, and the speaker was still focusing on Stieglitz and his work. Only the last fifteen minutes focused on O'Keeffe. Maybe we are just not meant to experience Georgia up close and personal. Or maybe, just maybe, we need another trip to Santa Fe.

THIRTY

Schooling 'In the Olden Days'

While in Frisco, Colorado, in 2015, Larry and I visited the two-room Dillon school house that had been built in 1883. Now a museum, it served as the town's main educational facility until 1910. Walking into that old building with its wooden floors, dusty chalkboards, and old-fashioned seats transported me back in time to my own experience in the 1950s in a two-room school house on the shores of Lake Champlain.

When my family moved to Keeseville, all classes from kindergarten to twelfth grade were held in a brick building on a hilltop on Main Street. It was built in 1936 and replaced the area's one-and two room school houses. By the mid-fifties, however, a growing population fueled by the expansion of near-by Plattsburgh Air Force base necessitated the construction of a new elementary school. In the meantime, classes were being held in temporary locations. My brother Jay spent fourth grade in the town's old shirt factory. Two years later, I was part of the group of students who were bussed the four miles to the two-room school house in Port Kent.

I am not sure how the teachers felt about being transported back in time one hundred years. Two wooden stoves provided the heat, the old oak floors were scuffed, and the bathrooms were far from modern. We students, however, loved it. The little red school house consisted of two huge rooms connecting a second and third grade class. Our lessons were punctuated with the sounds of train whistles from the Port Kent railroad station and horns from the ferries that transported cars to and from Burlington, Vermont. The school district transported our lunches, which we would eat at our desks. After lunch we would go outside for recess on a large grassy lot that overlooked Lake Champlain. On nice spring days, we walked to the nearby beaver dam for a 'mini' field trip.

We loved our second grade teacher, Mrs. Smith, who was sweet and kind and whose looks reminded me of the beautiful actress Loretta Young. My friend Julie had special memories of her. A left hander, Julie's first grade teacher tried to convert her until Julie's father set the teacher straight. Having a teacher like Mrs. Smith that accepted a southpaw was a relief.

Some of the students lived in Port Kent within walking distance of the school. One of my friends lived in a huge house right next to the railroad tracks. The trains went roaring past her front porch several times a day. I thought she was the luckiest person in the world to live so close to the train tracks. It was also while I was a student in Port Kent that I had my first heartbreak. I was in love with a young man who moved away at the end of second grade.

One of my clearest memories was our performing a play based on *Hansel and Gretel*. As I had been dressed as a witch that past Halloween, I got to play the villain to Julie's starring role as Gretel. In Act Two she pushed me into the "oven," a table covered in black construction paper with a drawing of the fireplace.

The next September, we started the school year in Port Kent. The elementary school was finished over the winter vacation, and we started classes there in January 1958. The new school was shiny and modern and beautiful. However, looking back, I have fonder recollections of my year and a half in that little red schoolhouse than I do about the new building.

Ironically, many years later, Adam and Julie had the opportunity to attend school in a similar building. Both children went to the Clifton Park Nursery School, housed an old red brick one room school house on the corner of Moe and Grooms Road. As a cooperative preschool, Larry and I participated as helping parents in Adam and Julie's classrooms. One of Julie's earliest memories is Larry coming in on Halloween as a clown with a big red honking nose. She thought she was the luckiest child in the world to have such a funny, talented father. Both children loved going to nursery school in that old building with its wooden floors, huge old windows, and parent-made shelves lining the walls filled with toys and books and arts and craft material.

Sylvie Rose's future elementary school in Frisco, a modern building with a huge playground, is only a few blocks from her home. I doubt if she will follow in the footsteps of her grandmother and mother. However, she will learn about the history of her small Rocky Mountain town: the Ute Indians who originally lived along its rivers, the mountain men who trapped beaver in this territory in the first half of the nineteenth century, the miners and their families who settled the town in the 1870s. She will enjoy picnics and concerts in the town's historic park, where she can play in original buildings that were once saloons, hotels, log homes, a jail and a chapel. And she can explore the nearby Dillon schoolhouse museum, with its wooden floors, dusty chalkboards, and wooden seats. And maybe then, Julie and I will share memories with Sylvie of our own little red schoolhouses.

THIRTY ONE

Traveling, Traveling—Looking for Something

For many years, friends had a sure-fire way to making sure their vacation would be perfect. They would call Larry and me to find out where and when we were going. Then they immediately chose *another* week and *another* location.

Our history of disastrous vacations dates back to our honeymoon in 1974. Twelve hours into our trip to Quebec City, Larry had a kidney stone attack. He spent five days flat on his back in a single bed in Jeffery Hale Hospital. I spent my days visiting with his French-speaking fellow patients and nurses and my nights sleeping in a decidedly non-honeymoon-like single bed in a nine dollar a night rooming house across the street.

The next year, we tried to take a second shot at a honeymoon by planning a trip to Nantucket. A hurricane hit Hyannis two hours before our ferry was supposed to leave for the island. We spent time at our friends' home in New Hampshire until the ferries were able to run again. The following year, on our third attempt, we 'vacationed' in Washington DC in the middle of a gale that knocked power out of most of the city, including our pricey hotel room.

Things didn't get much better after our kids were born. On a trip to Bar Harbor, Maine, the fog rolled in an hour after our arrival. Our view from our balcony was limited to the trees five feet from our hotel. Julie and I spent the entire time on a whale watch on the losing end of a battle with sea sickness. Four days later, the fog rolled out as we rolled out of the hotel parking lot on our way home.

The next three tries of getting away from it all with our family added to our share of disasters. In New Hampshire's White Mountains, Julie cut her foot the first night of our vacation. She didn't require stitches, but we spent the week carrying our seven-year-old daughter on our back. A trip to visit our parents in Fort Lauderdale ended with a flight delayed hours by a major snowstorm. In the Amish country, the temperature hit a record 103 degrees the second day we were there. Our vacation was limited to swimming in a small indoor pool and watching repeated showings of *An Officer and a Gentleman* in our hotel room.

Our trips to Cape Cod seemed to be punctuated by rain. Not an occasional drizzle with a few hours of sun in the afternoon. No. I mean the kind of rain that came down so hard, people were talking about building an ark. The deluge usually stopped just hours before Larry and I were going to kill each other after being imprisoned for several days in a small cabin with two bored, fighting children.

The ultimate family disaster vacation was our trip to Cape Cod in 1991. Our family arrived twelve hours before Hurricane Bob was supposed to hit North Carolina. The hurricane changed course with the eye of the storm hitting Cape Cod Canal. We spent the first full day in a shelter set up in an elementary school along with several hundred other stranded tourists.

When we finally got back to our cottage, the electricity was out, our outside shower was destroyed, and the grounds were coved with branches. We took heart in the weather forecaster's assurance that beautiful weather usually follows a hurricane. Unfortunately another front bringing two days of rain followed. The electricity and the sun returned only minutes after we had decided to pack in it as a lost cause and go home. The last two days, we shared the beach with swarms of angry homeless bees and wasps whose nests had been destroyed by the hurricane. The highlight of the vacation for me was buying a tee shirt that said, "I survived Hurricane Bob." I proudly wore it as a beach cover-up at the Cape for the next twenty years.

After that, our luck changed. In 1993, we went to California. We had nine days of perfect weather. Despite my fears of earthquakes, we didn't feel one tremor. We watched seals frolic in Monterey, drove through Big Sur, and walked for miles in San Francisco. Over the next few years, we had non-eventful, fun vacations with our children.

When Adam and Julie were in college, Larry and I tried cruising. The first two trips on luxury lines were wonderful, but the third had its problems. Rain and wind prevented us from going to two of our destinations. We had to take a detour to Guantanamo Bay to deliver a body of some poor individual who had died on board. President Bush declared war on Iraq. We got off the boat in Key West two hours late when two passengers failed to report to the mandatory immigration clearance. While two thousand other cruisers cooled their heels, the elderly couple were sunning themselves on their balcony. They were totally oblivious to the knocks on their doors and the public address system's request for "Mr. and Mrs. Finklestein in Cabin 732! Please report to the main dining room!" We would still be waiting to get off the boat if a crew member hadn't finally unlocked their door and rounded up the two culprits.

I don't know if our luck got better or if we—especially me!—began to accept the fact that one doesn't leave life and its ups and downs when one travels. So what if it rains buckets in the Galápagos Islands or it snows ten inches the first day of summer in the Rockies or if I compromise our credit card the first night in England. (Warning: Do not download books on your electronic reader through public WiFi!). We are grateful to have the time and resources to see the world. We just come prepared. We'll pack the necessary clothing along with a first aid kit, flashlights, our health insurance and traveler's insurance cards, and emergency instructions for hurricanes, lightning storms, gales, and blizzards. Finally, I pack a traveler's prayer to G-d to "lead us in our desired destination in health and joy and peace and to bring us home in peace." Amen.

THIRTY TWO

What's in a Name? Marilyn Meets Marilyns on Her Life Path

Since I was old enough to remember, people have always associated my name with Marilyn Monroe. I am frequently asked if I was named after the blonde icon. And, to this day, when new acquaintances or telephone business contacts ask me to repeat my first name, I often say, "I'm Marilyn, like Marilyn Monroe." In truth, the former Norma Jean did not become famous until after I was born. I was named after my Aunt Mary, and my mother chose my specific name because she loved Marilyn Miller, who was one of the most popular Broadway and film stars of the 1920s and early 1930s.

Although not a popular name choice today, I have shared my name and life with several other Marilyns. When I was around five years old, our town held a beauty contest. A tall, blonde beauty named Marilyn was declared the winner. I remember feeling the sense of pride that I shared a name with Miss Keeseville 1956.

While going through Keeseville Central School, the only other Marilyn I knew was a classmate two years ahead of me. I always looked up to her as she was one of the sweetest, kindest, and most intelligent people I knew. In her senior year, Marilyn was named

Yearbook Queen, the honor given to the most well-liked, respected senior girl. Again, I felt lucky to have the same name in this case as the most popular girl in our small school.

While enrolled in the University at Albany, I ran into a few more Marilyns. A freshman suite mate named Marilyn became a close friend of my cousin Marsha. Forty-two years later, our paths crossed again at Marsha's sixtieth birthday party.

Where the "Marilyn" coincidences began to really pile up was in my early twenties. Larry and I met at a Purim party. While sharing hamantashen, we also shared family history. Larry had a sister named Marilyn Shapiro, who, like me, was the third child of four children and the second girl. To add to the confusion, my sister-in-law kept her maiden name when she married. The family distinguishes us by using of our middle names: Marilyn Pearl and Marilyn Renee. My preference is the tongue-in-cheek version: "The Original" and "The New and Improved."

When our daughter Julie got married in 2007, another Marilyn came into the family. Her in-laws are Bill Massman and, you guessed it, *Marilyn* Martynuk. Despite the geographic distance between Fort Collins Marilyn and me, we have become dear friends, and the four in-laws even rented a condo near Julie and Sam in Frisco, Colorado, the summer our granddaughter was born. We got used to answering to our name based on which husband was calling out to us. As this is Marilyn's second grandchild, she already had dibs on the moniker of Nana Marilyn. I am not sure what Sylvie Rose will be calling me when she starts talking, but for now, I will be Grandma Marilyn. It is my understanding from several of my friends who have duplicate names (Bernie and Bernie; Carole and Carol; Bill and Bill), grandchildren rarely have issues distinguishing between them.

During our move to Florida, another Marilyn came into our lives. When we wanted to learn more about the Jewish organizations in the community, we got in touch with the Shalom Club's Marilyn. When we met each other, we found out that we have another connection. For several years, Marilyn, now a retired nurse, volunteered at the Maccabean Games in Israel. In 1997, she and our daughter Julie were part of the United States delegation, Julie as a track and field athlete and Marilyn as a member of the medical team. While packing up our house for our move, Larry and I came across the 1997 Maccabean Games yearbook. There was Nurse Marilyn front and center in one of the pictures.

When I moved to our community in Florida, I joined a women's writing group. There I met my most recent Marilyn, a woman from England who is a children's book author. We refer to each other as British Marilyn and Yankee Marilyn, and everyone in the group understands.

While in Colorado during Julie's pregnancy, I would browse through the stack of baby books she and Sam had accumulated. One of my favorites was a well-thumbed baby name book. Since we were not to learn our granddaughter's name until she was born, I spent quite a bit of time looking through the paperback, trying to guess which ones sounded like potential winners. Of course, I had to check out the authors' take on my name. It was not exactly flattering. Despite the Miller and Monroe who had made the name popular in previous generations, the authors stated that this choice had lost its former "stardust." "Marilyn," they stated, "has none of the freshness or sparkle that would inspire a parent to use it for a millennial child."

It was Marilyn Monroe herself who said, "We are all of us stars, and we deserve to twinkle." Fortunately, I have known many stars named Marilyn, and they all have brought light and sparkle to my life.

THIRTY THREE

A Moving Story: Oy! The Stuff

Packing up our house and moving to a completely furnished one in Florida brought the reality of real estate home for Larry and me.

Although our last move was over thirty-six years ago, I felt we were up to the task. I proudly went through my newly created "To Do" list: I contacted moving companies three months in advance. I began weekly and then almost daily trips to CAPTAIN'S Treasures and the library to give away unwanted household goods and the over two hundred books we had collected on our bookshelves. Larry and I reached out to family and friends to find new homes for our Early American furniture. At the same time we were clearing out what we didn't need, we started packing up what I thought we *would* need.

And this is when reality hit. Even after selling, giving away, and donating carloads of our life, we still had much more than we had ever imagined. Bath and Body Works Cherry Blossom shower gel; shoe horns from Larry's parents' store; nutcrackers and picks; scissors; supermarket totes, Special Olympics tee shirts—you name it, and we had duplicates and triplicates and more. We upped the amount we were NOT taking. Like the all-consuming plant Audrey in *Little Shop of Horrors,* however, the amount of stuff continued to grow. We purchased more moving boxes from Home Depot and more bubble wrap, tape, "Fragile" labels, and wrapping paper from Staples, and we kept packing and packing and packing. And we hadn't yet touched the "essentials" from our kitchen, bath, and bedroom.

Miraculously, by a week before our move, almost all of the packing was completed. I doubled checked the boxes to make sure they were securely sealed, numbered them with a thick marker, and inventoried them in a notebook. When I got to my one hundred and thirtieth box, I began to "real"-ly panic. We even opened up boxes to find items to leave behind. By that point, however, we knew most of it was going to be loaded on the moving van.

When Allied Van Lines arrived for their pick-up that sunny, warm June morning, even they were a little overwhelmed with the number of boxes. It took three men three hours to load it all on the truck, along with my piano, two dressers, a chair, and a garbage can filled with garden tools, mops, and brooms. By noon, Larry and I said one last good-bye to our home. I sobbed loudly on the shoulders of my neighbors who had gathered to send us off, and we started the two and a half day drive down to Florida

We arrived in the evening of June 3 and were able to quickly unpack what we brought down in our cars: our suitcases; pillows; sheets for the king-sized bed; a couple of towels; two of each of plates and silverware, wine glasses, regular glasses; two knives, two pots, a corkscrew, and a bottle of wine. After a quick trip to Publix for fruit, vegetables, milk, bread, salmon, and veggies, we were good to go. It was like being newlyweds. By that time, we figured out we should have left almost everything home as we already had more than enough to survive. Four days later, the van and our 130 boxes arrived.

Within hours, we were both buried in bubble wrap. While I unloaded the kitchen boxes, Larry took care of the clothes and the rest of our household goods. I cursed myself out loud: "How did I manage to bring so much when I thought I gave so much away?" Larry saved his comments for under-his-breath rants. "We aren't going to need long underwear in Florida!" or "I thought we weren't bringing the pancake griddle!" or "When did we acquire two hundred Broadway musical CDs?"

When our realtors came over with a bottle of wine on the second day of unpacking, they suggested that we (1) drink the wine. The entire bottle. Immediately; (2) empty all the boxes as soon as possible to "motivate" us to get settled more quickly; and (3) pile all the empty boxes in the garage so they could give them to another client who was moving. Larry took this advice much too seriously. As I continued to methodically empty the kitchen boxes and place the items on the cabinet shelves, Larry emptied every remaining box and piled all the contents on every bit of available space in the living room, office, and second bath. If that wasn't upsetting enough, he had unloaded all the linens, sheets, pillows, and blankets on the bed in the guest room. When I walked into the room, I felt I was reliving *The Princess and the Pea.* The pile reached to the ceiling fan. I was so angry I almost slept in guest bed that night, but I couldn't climb on top of the mess.

In the end, our move was successful. We actually had most of our boxes unpacked and organized by the end of the first week. Soon after, a Salvation Army truck picked up around fifteen boxes of items we didn't need. We knew we would eventually have to deal with the excess pictures that we brought and had stacked in the second bedroom, but at least we were settled in all the other rooms. And the only things we misplaced in the move were my Weight Watchers charms and two boxes of toothpicks, both which we found six months later. Not bad, considering.

Still, in hindsight, our *"real*ity" experience is a cautionary tale for all my friends and relatives who are considering a move. Follow the same advice savvy travelers give: Pack only half of what you think you need and leave the rest behind. Meanwhile, if anyone needs a slightly dusty but usable pancake griddle, six pairs of long underwear or a *Fiddler on the Roof* CD, contact me. I will be sitting on our lanai in my tank top, my favorite pair of shorts, and my Tevas, sipping wine from a huge travel goblet, the only things I needed to pack for our new home in Florida in the first place.

THIRTY FOUR

Shaking Up the Familiar: New Home Means New Favorite Spots

Up until June 2015, Larry and I always occupied the same seats at Congregation Beth Shalom in Clifton Park. We always sat in the fourth row, left side of the *bima*, on the two end seats. The Arnolds were on the middle aisle, the Grossmans were next to them, and the Toubs sat behind us.

There was a reason for our seating choice. First of all, Larry and I wanted to sit near our friends. Second of all, Larry liked the end seats so we could get out easily if we needed to take a break. Finally one of two memorial boards were next to us, and we sat right next to the plaques we had gotten in memory of our parents and an uncle. That was our spot every Shabbat service we attended for innumerable years. Sometimes, we would arrive late and someone else would have taken "our" seats. I am not sure if they felt our angry glare burning a hole in the back of their heads. It would have served them right!

Having one's spot is ingrained in our brains from our earliest years in school. We were given seats in elementary school, but it was even more formal in the upper grades when we were always seated alphabetically. In home room, I, Marilyn Cohen, sat behind the same person from seventh through twelfth grade, the same place we were assigned in many of our classes. He wore shirts with a loop in the middle under the seam, and I remember grabbing it and trying to pull it off. I thought my attempt at flirting was cute, but I am sure his parents didn't like the fact that he was coming home with holes in the back of those nice button downs.

However, even when we are not assigned seats, humans, by habit, tend to choose the same place out of a psychological need. In his book *Maximizing Project Success Through Human Performance*, industrial psychologist Bernardo Tirado gives this action a name, *seat marking*. It is a way in which we humans unconsciously mark our territory." Think of how many years you sat in assigned seats in school," says Dr. Tirado. "That level of conditioning continues into our adulthood, even though our seats are no longer assigned."

Larry and I certainly haven't outgrown the habit. We eat in our "assigned seats" at our dinner table; we often request the same table and same chairs at a favorite restaurant; we sleep on the same sides of the bed no matter where we are. And when I go to one of my exercise classes, I choose the same spot on the dance floor to follow the instructor. I like to be in the second row in the middle with a clear view of the mirror.

Of course, all this territoriality does cause problems. While taking a Zumba class at the YMCA just before our move, I chose the one empty spot in the first row. A minute before the class was to start, a woman took her place next to me, literally jamming herself into my left arm. "Excuse me," I said. "I am standing here."

"No, this is my spot," she informed me, and refused to budge. We almost came to blows until I found an empty space in the back of the room.

In our new home, I have a quiet retreat. Larry and I purchased a glider that sits on the open part of the lanai, between the two ferns the former owners left for us. With a cup of Earl Grey tea in my hand, I can leisurely watch the bird and animal life that are visiting our pond on that particular day. Not since I was a teenager, when I sat on the rocks on Willsboro Point with its beautiful view of Lake Champlain and Burlington, Vermont, have I had a particular place where I can find such peace and contentment.

Now that we have moved to Florida, I don't know who sits in our seats at our Clifton Park *shul*. Has another couple moved into our spot, or are those two blue chairs sitting empty, waiting patiently for us to return? We are still new at Congregation Shalom Aleichem in Kissimmee and haven't settled into the place in which we sit on a regular basis. On the first day of Rosh Hashanah, we found empty seats a few rows back next to a couple we had met, and Wendy saved those seats for us for each of the Yom Kippur services. We are still deciding if that place continues to work out for us.

After the morning Rosh Hashanah services, two other couples joined us for a holiday meal. We finished the chopped liver, crackers and Manischewitz wine in the breakfast nook and moved on to the chicken in mushroom sauce, *kasha varnishkes*, and honeyed carrots at the dining room table. One of my friends asked, "Where do you and Larry usually sit?" Larry and I looked at each other questioningly. This was the first time we had ever even eaten in the dining room and had no idea where our usual spots were. But Larry gravitated to the head of the table, and I chose the seat closest to the kitchen. We all settled into place, said a *haMotzi*, the traditional prayer over bread, and began our meal. Larry and I had found our spots, and our new house felt more like our home.

THIRTY FIVE

Home Town Tours

A number of years ago, Larry's sister Carole had her annual Fourth of July party in her backyard in Saratoga Springs. What made this party special is that our niece and her significant other had made the trip up from Virginia, the first time he had ever been to Saratoga County.

Katie wanted to show Swamy around the city, and Larry offered to give the tour. We piled into the Prius, Larry behind the wheel with Swamy next to him for the best view. Katie and I took seats in the back, and we began our excursion.

Larry's first stop was not the race track or the Hall of Springs or Congress Park. Nope. He immediately drove to Avery Street and parked outside a white two-story colonial. "This is where Katie's mother grew up," Larry explained. "I spent hours playing stoop ball right there on those front steps."

When Katie and I suggested that Larry show Swamy more of Saratoga Springs tourist spots, he assured us he was getting there. But the next stop was in front of another house down the street. "That is where our piano teacher lived," he offered. "His wife was my fourth grade teacher."

My niece and I began to giggle. We knew where this was going.

Our next stop was in front of one of the gates at the race track, where Larry sold newspapers and, when he turned eighteen, beer and hot dogs to the patrons. This site was accompanied by a story as to how Larry was once accused of not having the exact amount of money at the end of the day, and how he had proven his honesty to the manager. We saw the field where Larry played baseball into the summer nights, his old high school, and the outer limits of his newspaper route.

Swamy did get to see a little of the true tourist places but only as we drove by on Larry's sentimental tour of the "real" Saratoga Springs. By the end of the hour, Katie and I were laughing out loud. Swamy, who is a sweet gentle soul, smiled throughout and offered an occasional "Very nice!"

Recently, I shared this story with my friend Marcie. Rather than thinking it was funny, she told me that she totally got it. Completely. Marcie had grown up in Boston, and after her daughter graduated Northeastern, she insisted that the two of them take a tour of the "real" Boston. Marcie drove her daughter to her old synagogue Agudath Israel, the house where her father had lived in the once thriving Jewish neighborhood of Dorchester, and her old school, Girls Latin. "My daughter thought that she knew Boston because she had been to Fenway Park and walked the Freedom Trail," said Marcie. "But she knew nothing unless I introduced her to the Boston that was my home."

It then hit me that one's home town, no matter how heralded or how small, was not about the tourist spots. It was about memories. Keeseville is just a dot on the map. When Larry first visited me in my home town in 1973, I didn't bring him to Ausable Chasm, our one claim to fame. He and I took a walk over the swinging bridge and the steep steps up to Pleasant Street. We circled around past my old high school. I pointed out the church right across the street. "When I was a child, all my Catholic friends crossed themselves when they walked past it," I told him. "I did it for a while until my parents explained to me that Jews 'didn't do that.'" Then we walked home over the keystone bridge.

For over thirty-six years we did similar tours for our out-of-area Clifton Park guests. No visit would be complete without a drive past the little red school house where my children went to nursery school, a walk through the Vischer Ferry Wildlife Preserve, and a stop for apple cider donuts at Riverview Orchards in the fall or ice cream at the Country Drive-in in the summer. None of these places would be in *Lonely Planet* or even local "What To See" guides in the Capital Region. To us, however, they represent what is best in our hometown. Not to say that we wouldn't bring guests to the State Museum or the Saratoga Battlefield or even Cooperstown. However, when it comes to important, we know.

Our home in Florida is less than forty minutes from Disney World. Lego Land and Sea World are even closer. When guests come, I am sure that these world-famous attractions may be on top of their 'must see' list. But after only few months, we already had selected off the grid locations, starting with the view of Pacers Pond from our lanai. On the first day of Rosh Hashanah, Larry and I woke up to the sight of four birds, two lizards, and an alligator that Larry named Brutus, whose size rivals anything one can see in Gatorland. We found a great custard stand down the road, and the Disney Wilderness Preserve is only four miles away.

So, my dear Larry, now I 'get it' too. You showed Swamy the best that Saratoga Springs had to offer you, and I know you will do the same for our future Florida visitors. Just warn them about Brutus before they step out into our back yard.

THIRTY SIX

Exercising My Options

Growing up in upstate New York in the 1950s, I never thought much about exercise. I walked to and from school every day, swam in Lake Champlain in the summer, and biked leisurely through the apple orchards outside of town. A couple of my close friends played on a girl's intramural softball team. With my hand-eye coordination, I wisely sat on the bench and watched. And gym class? All I remember were those ugly red bloomers we were forced to wear while hurling ourselves over the saddle horses or jumping on a trampoline while our classmates "protected us" by standing along the sides. (I bet that form of exercise is not part of any gym class in this century!)

It was not until I married Larry that I actually began to incorporate regular exercise into my daily routine. Larry was a high school runner. Once he began working for New York State, he met up with a group every day at lunch to do a loop around the State Campus. Although I had no interest in pounding the pavement, his interest in keeping fit encouraged me to do something every day: a bike ride, a walk; video work-outs with Jane Fonda, Charlene Prickett, and Step Reebok.

Over the years, we expanded our exercise options. Around 1990, we purchased our first of several road bikes on which we racked thousands of miles riding throughout Saratoga and Albany country.

While living in Clifton Park, we faithfully rode the stationary bike that was in our family room, albeit with two different mindsets. Larry was intense and focused, pushing the limits of the resistance and rotation settings. I, on the other hand, viewed it as a great way to get to watch movies or reruns of *The Big Bang Theory* while getting in my mileage. To be honest, I tried to bike when he wasn't home to avoid his encouraging me to "go faster." If he did walk into the room, I sped up and started gasping for air. That usually placated him enough to convince him I was working out. Once he left the room, I slowed down and got back to my show.

We also took advantage of the Pacific Fitness trainer that we had set up in our basement in 1996. Larry used it three times a week barring injury or travel. Even though I knew weight training is important for post-menopausal women, I used it in fits and stops, making excuses. After all, I reasoned, I am not interested in winning a Mrs. Universe contest! When I joined the YMCA a few years before we moved. I decided at that point that Zumba and kickboxing classes were enough for toning. For the most part, however, we certainly got our money's worth out of most of our fitness purchases.

Not to say we haven't had a couple of misses. The most obvious failure was my purchase of two hula hoops. One was the classic 1950s plastic design. The other, at the suggestion of my Weight Watcher's instructor, was a super deluxe weighted model. No matter how hard I tried, I never got beyond one rotation on either hoop. Larry, however, was a natural, and he showed off his incredible hip action several times before I gave both hoops to our six-year-old great-niece. She, like Larry, was a natural.

Larry and I had different approaches to keeping track of our exercise. Larry has always used pre-measured running routes and the cyclometer on his bike. For ten years I used a clunky pedometer that attached to my waist band to track my daily steps, especially on long trips where we do a great deal of hiking. I once had to retrieve it when I left it on the plane after a six-hour cross-country flight. The flight attendant's wry comment? "Bet you didn't rack up many steps flying over the Great Plains."

A few years ago, I was given a Fitbit Zip, a compact step/mile tracking device that clipped to my bra. When synched with my iPhone, it gave me progress updates on my 10,000 step-a-day goal. One day, I was in my kitchen when my phone dinged. "Congratulations! You have reached your goal of 10,000 steps!" read the banner. My initial thrill of accomplishment was quickly squelched when I realized I wasn't even *wearing* my Fitbit. I had reached my goal because I had left the device on the clothes dryer. The vibrations from the machine gave me a quick, easy, no-sweat 8000 steps—No, I *didn't* count it. Soon after this incident, I forgot to unclip the Fitbit from my sports bra, and I washed it along with the rest of my laundry. Goodbye, Fitbit! I replaced it with a more expensive model that was worn on the wrist, thus avoiding another wash day wipe-out.

While wearing the Fitbit on a trip to Jamaica, I averaged around 12,000 steps a day by morning walks around the hilly grounds and by participation in pool volleyball games. I'd love to tell you that I came back thinner, but I guess all that walking didn't negate the five course dinners, the wine, and the chocolate martinis for dessert. It took me a few weeks to lose the seven pounds I gained.

One of the features that attracted us to our home in Florida were the miles of bike and walking trails, two large fully equipped fitness centers, and numerous swimming pools where I can do laps. We left all our equipment behind except our outdoor bikes. And my Fitbit. Like Pavlov's dog, I have become addicted the ding of my iPhone that lets me know I reached my goal. Speaking of which, I am currently five hundred steps short and it's eleven o'clock at night. Time to quit writing and start jogging in place.9501, 9502 9503......

THIRTY SEVEN

Rose and Me: A Story of Friendship

Friendships can happen at any age. I met Rose Calderon when I was 61 and she was 99. It was a beginning of a lovely relationship that lasted until her passing two years later.

I met Rose through a twist of fate. Doris Calderon, a friend and member of our synagogue, had been diagnosed with Myeloid Dysplastic Syndrome, a rare form of blood cancer, in March 2010. After months of chemotherapy and medical setbacks, Doris had found a donor match and was scheduled for stem cell transplant at Sloan Kettering during the winter of 2012. Treatments required that she and her husband Marty stay in New York City during the procedure.

In preparation, Doris sent out an update through email to her friends and family. "Many people have asked how they can help," she wrote, "and I just need two things. Someone needs to water my plants, and other people need to visit my mother-in-law Rose while we are in New York City." I quickly wrote back, "I will kill your plants, but I promise I won't kill your mother-in-law."

A few days later, Doris and I met each other in Rose's room at Daughters of Sarah Nursing Home. Rose was not immediately receptive. "I don't even know you," she said. "Why are you coming to visit me?" I explained to Rose that I wanted to help Doris and Marty, and we might just become friends.

So in February 2012, I started visiting Rose once a week. Her defensive armor quickly softened, and we found much to talk about. She told me about her parents' home on Nantucket, her move to New York City to find a job during the Depression, her love of dancing, her falling in love a little too quickly with a handsome man who also loved to dance, and her raising two children on her own after her separation and divorce. I shared stories about my own parents, about my marriage and my children, and about my travels. As the weeks went by, our friendship grew, and my weekly visits continued even after Doris and Marty came home, thankfully returning in July 2012 with good news of a successful transplant.

And those visits were helping me in my own grieving process. My father had passed away in 2008; my mother, in 2011. While neither death was unexpected, their absence certainly left a hole in my heart, which time with Rose was filling.

As the weeks went by, I got to know the staff and the residents of her unit. The activity director asked me if I would like to read to the residents. Over the next eighteen months, my visits with Rose were followed by thirty minute sessions in which I would share articles, poems, even Ann Lander columns with a cluster of residents who gathered around me in the general meeting area.

Rose wasn't always happy that she had to "share me." She also felt the group sessions were a waste of my time. "Most of those people can't hear you," she argued, "and even if they could, they usually fall asleep!" She repeated that line every week, but I kept saying that they enjoyed it. One day, after Rose repeated usual complaint, I tried to prove her wrong. I turned to another resident who had attended my group for several months. "Hannah, you've been coming to my little sessions for a while," I said. "Do you enjoy it?" Hannah looked shocked. "I don't know what you are talking about!" she said. "I just moved here yesterday! I've never seen you before in my life!" Rose just smiled and said, "See?" Soon after that, with the help and guidance of the unit's activity director, I spent my extra time on individual visits, talking not only to the residents who gravitated to the common areas but also to those who preferred just to stay in their rooms

In August 2013, Rose celebrated her 100th birthday with a party thrown by the family outside at Daughters of Sarah. Rose looked especially radiant and happy that day as, along with staff and friends from the facility, she was surrounded by her children, grandchildren, and great-grandchildren.

After her hundredth birthday, Rose's health declined. She was confined to a wheelchair; her vision deteriorated even further, and she could barely hear. "I've lived long enough," she would say to me. "I wish God would take me." As she approached 101, my visits with Rose became shorter as she would fall asleep or just say, "I'm tired. We'll visit next week."

Just before Larry and I left for a trip to Europe, Rose and I chatted about my upcoming itinerary and her upcoming 101st birthday. She wished me a good trip, and I promised to send postcards from England and Greece. When I came back, I talked to Rose in between her falling asleep. I wheeled her over to lunch, where she struggled to eat her ground-up food. On what was to be my last visit, Rose was lying peacefully in her bed in a semi-conscious state. As I held her hand, I told her that I loved her and that I was grateful for our friendship. When I kissed her forehead, I knew it was for the last time. "Have a safe journey, Rose," I whispered.

Two weeks later, while visiting my children in Colorado, I got word from a friend that Rose had passed away that morning. We both agreed it was a blessing. Rose had had a long, full life, and she was so tired and so ready. I shed some tears, shared the news with Larry, and talked about our unique friendship. A few minutes later, I opened up my Facebook page, and her grandchildren had posted tributes and pictures, including one of Rose on her 100th birthday. Goodbye, Rose! Safe journey!

THIRTY EIGHT

Tossing the Appliances and Making Cookies

I am not a foodie, and I certainly am not Julia Childs. However, I enjoy my time in the kitchen. I have a few favorite standbys that I whip up frequently: spinach lasagna roll-ups, chicken in wine sauce, a hearty minestrone soup. The one dessert I am known for are what my friends have tagged "Marilyn's World Famous Chocolate Chip Cookies." I cannot figure out what makes them so special as I just use the recipe on the back of Nestle's Tollhouse chocolate chips package. But somehow, I am always asked to bring them whenever I am sharing a meal with family and friends. In 2015, they had to be especially good, because my World Famous Cookies were also going to be the World's Most Expensive.

Chocolate chip cookie batter works best when prepared with a full-stand mix master so that the butter and sugar are properly creamed and the batter is sufficiently mixed. For over twenty-five years, I used my mother's Sunbeam that she purchased in the 1950s and that I inherited when they moved out of our big house in Keeseville in 1981. As was typical of appliances of that era, that machine got me through numerous batches of cookies and sponge cakes and mandelbrodt. In 2001, however, the motor stopped working, and the technicians at our favorite small appliance repair shop said it was no longer worth fixing.

On the advice of my friend Lynn, a master baker, I replaced the machine with a KitchenAid. For the next thirteen years, the appliance, like its predecessor, faithfully churned out my limited repertoire of culinary delights. One day, however, when I was using the mixer to make a marble Bundt cake, I realized the machine had only one speed: Spin-So-Fast-That-the-Batter-Flies- Out-of-the-Bowl-Onto-the-Walls speed.

I loaded the mixer into my car's trunk and drove to appliance repair shop to drop it off to be repaired. To my surprise, I found the store, a possible victim of our throw-away-and-just-buy-new mentality, closed up tight. My Yellow Pages and internet search for small appliance repair people also came up empty-handed. I did, however, find websites that included YouTube videos for do-it-yourselfers. "Hey," I thought to myself. "We're retired! We have time, and we certainly can fix this machine ourselves."

I ordered the two parts in question from the Internet. The first, the mixer sensor, was only six dollars and was considered by our YouTube expert as a minor fix. The second part, a fairly expensive speed control board, was recommended in case the simple fix didn't work. I reasoned that always could return it if we fixed the mixer with the less expensive part.

Although we purchased the parts soon after it broke, I found over the next few months multiple excuses for not making the repair. I was on yet another diet and not baking as much. I found a simple one-bowl brownie recipe that required just a spoon. When I had company for dinner, I asked my guests to bring the dessert. However, that November friends extended an invitation to their annual latke dinner, and they were insistent that I bring my World Famous Chocolate Chip Cookies. We had procrastinated long enough.

A few days later, Larry and I pulled up the mix master from the basement, the parts from the hall closet, and the laptop from the office. We turned on the YouTube video and began disassembling the mixer to get to the area in which we believed the speed belt was housed.

After twenty minutes of unscrewing every screw on the top of the machine, we found a different video that expanded the disassembly. Another ten minutes and several tries later, we were still no closer to finding where to put the &*!@ belt. We searched the Internet again, found another video, and started taking apart another component of the machine. By that time, there was grease on the tablecloth, on our hands, and on our clothes. The table was covered with over a hundred parts, nuts, and bolts. Eureka moment: the parts I had purchased were for a newer model than the one we were going to fix. And even if the replacement parts fit into the machine, we, like all the king's horses and all the king's men, didn't know how to put all the pieces back together again.

"I know you hate to get appliances for Chanukah," said Larry. "But if you allow me to dump this whole mess into the garbage bin, you can just purchase a new one"

"Agreed," I said.

We threw the mess that used to be a stand mixer into the trash, After some time researching replacements, I ordered through the internet a beautiful deluxe KitchenAid in espresso, one of the fifteen color options available. We were back in the cookie baking business before our Chanukah dinner.

Between the parts (that were only exchangeable within thirty days) and the new mixer, we invested over $400 to make the first batch of five dozen cookies. I brought cookies and cakes to several more Clifton Park events until I brought the KitchenAid down to Florida. My cookies are favorites down here as well. "These are the best chocolate chip cookies I've tasted since my mother made them in Buffalo fifty years ago," one friend commented. Hopefully, my new mixer will be churning them out for many years to come.

THIRTY NINE

Making Peace with Noise

On the lanai in our new home, Larry and I have a large set of wind chimes that make beautiful sounds with the slightest breeze. One morning I had a Shalom Club board meeting at my home. The patio door was open, and I commented to those gathered around the dining room table that I never get tired of hearing the music. "It's fine during the day," one of the board members commented. "But have any of your neighbors complained? I had to ask my neighbors to take theirs down as I was losing sleep!"

How ironic that I never gave it a thought, I who has struggled with noise most of my adult life.

It certainly wasn't a problem when I was young. Our house in Keeseville backed up to bowling alley on the right and lumber yard to the left. Often times the lumber trucks would come in at 2 am. And the noises of the pins crashing in the bowling alley? That was constant. In addition, we lived less than fifteen miles from Plattsburgh Air Force Base, and the jets flew over our house all the time. I never heard them, never thought anything about them.

When my parents purchased a cottage on Lake Champlain in 1966, we were lulled to sleep each night by the sound of crickets. Guests from the city who stayed overnight complained, but to me it was a symphony. When I went to college, the dorm was always noisy. Radios blared, people stomped upstairs, and parties went on into the wee hours on the weekends. In addition, our campus was a scant few miles from the Albany airport. Planes were flying over our dorms and our classrooms all day. Did I hear any of that? Never.

With all this history of noise, you would think I would have been totally desensitized. The apartments that followed, first with a former college roommate and later in our first two years of marriage, had just the occasional sound of footsteps overhead.

In 1976, Larry and I bought our first home, a nice raised ranch on a quiet street in Halfmoon. The first night we moved in, we opened our bedroom windows to get some fresh air and were hit with a wall of noise. As we looked out into the darkness, we saw the headlights of the cars flickering through the trees. What we hadn't realized when we bought the house was that we were less than a half a mile from the Northway. The sound from the cars varied from a low background hum during the day to a cacophony of sounds during the rush hour. The winter cold exacerbated the volume. The worst time was in the summer when the windows were open. We could even hear trucks changing gears.

It would be wonderful if I could say that I handled this with calm and fortitude, but I fixated on the noise. Despite a large backyard and a big flower garden, I spent as little time outside as possible. During the day, I kept the doors and windows shut and turned up the volume on the radio or the television. At night, we turned on the window air conditioner in our bedroom so we didn't have to open the windows. Within two years, we put the house up for sale and began to look for a quieter spot in Clifton Park.

On a warm September afternoon, our realtor showed us a home on a quiet cul-de-sac two miles west of the Northway. The front lawn was plush and green, the skies were blue, and a cute squirrel lopped its way across the expansive front yard. The back yard backed up to a quiet wooded area, and the house was immaculate on the inside. We put a bid on it the next day.

A week later, I made arrangements for my mother-in-law to see the home. While we were waiting for the realtor, we saw a plane fly over our heads on its way to the Albany Airport. It was so low that we could read the American Airlines insignia on its side and see the wheels descend as the pilot prepared for their descent. "My goodness," my mother-in-law exclaimed. "You thought the Northway was bad! How in the world are you going to handle the planes?"

As soon as I was near a phone, I called Larry and burst into tears. "We are on a flight pattern!" I cried. "The plane noise is worse than the noise from the Northway. We can't buy this house!" Larry tried to calm me down. It was too late to go back on the contract, and I felt as if I was going from the frying pan into the fire.

Over the thirty-six years we lived there, I made peace with the planes. As a matter of fact, that last morning, when I said goodbye to our neighbors before we started our 1300 mile trip to our new home, I cried like a baby, wondering how in the world I could leave our quiet cul-de-sac behind.

Larry and I drove down to Florida and pulled into the driveway of our new home on an early June evening. The house was closed up, and the air conditioning was on full blast to counter the summer heat and humidity. We unpacked the suitcases and boxes and wine we had brought down with us to settle in a bit before the moving van was to arrive three days later. By 10 o'clock, we were tired and ready for some down time. We poured two glasses of wine and opened up the doors to our lanai. We were hit with a wall of noise.

"What in the world is that?" Larry said. It took us a couple of minutes for us to realize that the roar was coming from the nature preserve behind our home. We had arrived at the height of mating season in Central Florida, and we were hearing tree frogs, alligators, wild boars, and goodness knows what other animals lurked in the wildlife preserve behind our house. The noise was louder than any college dorm, any expressway, any flight pattern we had ever heard.

But somehow this was different. This was the noise nature made, similar to the sounds I heard on Lake Champlain years before. I started laughing, and I gave Larry a hug. "We're home!" I said. "L'chaim!" And we clinked our glasses and toasted our new home, our new life, our new adventure.

FORTY

Does History Repeat Itself?

As Larry and I settle into our new life in Florida, it is interesting to compare our new life in Central Florida to my parents' retirement years near Fort Lauderdale.

When the last of the Cohen children headed for college, my parents spent a couple of weeks each winter in Florida. When they retired, they sold the house in Keeseville and moved into their cottage on Lake Champlain. They escaped to Florida for two or three months in the dead of winter, splitting their time between short-term rentals and relatives' pull-out couches. In time, they purchased a one-bedroom condo in Hawaiian Gardens, a complex in Lauderdale Lakes that they had heard about through a cousin.

After years of living in a community with lots of snow and with few Jewish people, they thrived in the sunshine and in the company of *Yiddishkeit*, fellow Jews who had moved to the Sunshine State from New York City and Long Island. Their lives fell into a pattern. They shopped at Publix and went to their doctors' appointments in the morning. By noon, they joined all the other retirees by the small community pool. The women splashed around in the water while the men kibitzed on their beach chairs under large umbrellas. The conversation consisted of bad jokes, condo gossip, politics, and

161

discussions as to which restaurants offered the best early bird specials. My mother had grown up speaking Yiddish to her parents, and my father knew a few expressions, so they started a popular Yiddish Club that met once a week. Dad played poker; Mom went to flea markets with friends.

Outside of my father's occasional game of golf, my parents got their exercise walking back and forth to the pool. Deerfield Beach was only a half an hour away, but my father hated the sun, the heat, and the sand. As a result, my mother, who didn't drive in Florida, limited her visits to the ocean to when her children could take her when we visited.

Hawaiian Gardens offered entertainment in the clubhouse, usually a singer or a comedian who had worked on the Borscht Belt. The performers weren't paid a great deal, many were a little beyond their prime, and the audience could be downright cruel. During one of our visits, a woman singer was belting out Broadway tunes. When she asked if the audience would like her to do an encore, one of the residents yelled out, "No! You're terrible! Get off the stage!"

Larry and I flew down at least once a year and joined them in their routine. In the morning, I would take my mother to the supermarket or the flea market. At noon, we headed to the pool. At three o'clock, no matter how beautiful the weather, we all went upstairs to get ready to leave their apartment by four o'clock for that day's early bird special. The meals varied in quality, but there was tons of food with enough leftovers, extra bread, lemon slices, and a few Sweet 'n Low packets to take home for the next day's lunch. Even when they relocated to a larger condo, their routine remained the same. And their lives always included visits from relatives and friends from New York as well as get-togethers with new friends they had made.

Although we enjoyed our visits, Larry and I could not picture ourselves living the sedentary East Coast Florida condo life that my parents enjoyed. When we moved to our adult active community in Central Florida, we felt we had found our own piece of heaven that quite different from my parents' situation. Our home sat on a large scenic lot with plenty of room for family and friends to visit. Our community had two community recreational centers where I could take exercise classes and swim laps. Larry could play pickleball. We had miles of neighborhood streets where we could take long walks and longer bike rides. Many clubs and groups offered us innumerable ways to meet people from around the country and the world. Many of the activities revolved around the synagogue and the Shalom Club, but we also participated in club activities offered by groups with ties to Italy, England, the Caribbean, and Western Upstate New York. We had a full, diverse life.

Once we lived here for a few months, however, I realized how much we have in common with my parents. We go to the pool and pickleball courts to visit with friends. We often head to our favorite restaurant by four o'clock so we can beat the crowds. Recent entertainment included a headliner from the Sixties whose toupee and fancy tux didn't cover the fact that his body and voice were not what they were fifty years ago. The ocean is only ninety minutes away, but we don't feel like fighting the traffic. We share a great deal of time with our family and our old friends from around the country. And, like my parents, we plan on escaping the summer heat by spending time in Frisco, Colorado. It's not Lake Champlain, but at 9100 feet it certainly beats Florida's summers.

When my daughter and son-in-law recently visited us, they repeatedly told us how glad they were that that we were so happy here. However, they also said they wouldn't choose this lifestyle. If they were fortunate enough to have life after full-time employment, they wanted small mountain towns and ski trails. I hope wherever they live, they will enjoy sunny skies, good health, lots of activities to keep busy. Most importantly, I hope they encounter many relatives and old and new friends with whom to share their time.

FORTY ONE

Home Is Where They Can't Throw You Out

My tears started as soon as the plane's wheels hit the Albany airport runway that cold, crisp morning before Thanksgiving.

I didn't expect it. Sure, there were tears when Larry and I locked the front door of our home in Clifton Park for the last time. But we had settled fairly quickly into our new community in Florida, had made friends, had joined clubs. We had said repeatedly that our relocating to an active 55 plus community in Central Florida was one of the best decisions we had ever made in our lives.

We had visited our daughter, son-in-law, and granddaughter in Colorado in late October. The timing was right for going back to Saratoga County to spend Thanksgiving with Larry's siblings and their families as we had done so many years in the past. Fortunately for us, friends were spending the week in California and generously offered us their car and their home for the week, making the stay that much easier.

The Sunday before Thanksgiving, we packed our bags with clothes that had been stuffed in the back of our closet: sweaters, our Polar Plunge sweatshirts, long underwear, packable winter jackets, mittens and gloves. Monday morning, we rode to the airport in jeans and long sleeves and put on sweaters just before we got on the plane.

Two and a half hours later, we began our descent into the airport. We looked over the plane's wings and picked out familiar spots: the Empire State Plaza where Larry had spent most of his working career; the place along the river where I first began working at the Capital District Educational Opportunity Center, and my alma mater, University at Albany. It was seeing those buildings, those places so linked to our lives in the Capital District, that made me realize that I was coming home.

While waiting for the shuttle to take us to the lot where our friends' car was parked, we both agreed that our bodies, after months of sunshine and eighty degree temperatures, were not used to the cold. It didn't stop us from checking out our favorite old haunts while near Wolf Road: a favorite jeweler, a favorite Chinese restaurant for lunch. We stopped at Colonie Center to find a couple of Chanukah gifts. While there, we ran into an old work/running friend of Larry's. Jim and his wife knew we had moved. We connected as if it were just a casual meeting not separated by over six months.

That night, we met friends for dinner at the Dinosaur BBQ. The minute Sue and I hugged each other, my tears began again. We had been two of the "Three Amigas" for over thirty years. We had lost one of us to cancer less than a month before our Florida move. Sue and I immediately had the same impression Larry and I had experienced earlier that day—we were just catching up after a short break from each other. It was so good to spend an evening with old friends and to catch up on our lives in person.

Larry and I jammed into our visit as many Capital Region experiences that we could into our week stay. We drank apple cider and bit into honey crisp apples (Florida's apples are an extremely weak substitute for our North Country apples). We drove our old cycling route on Riverview Road and took a walk in Kinns Road Park. We shared several meals, including Thanksgiving, with Larry's family. On Sunday, we saw our great nephew play ice hockey.

In between, we visited friends and got caught up on their lives.

One couple shared the news that they were expecting their first grandchild; another, their first great grandchild. Larry's closest friend and his wife had just come back from Kentucky, and we shared grandchildren stories while eating barbecue chicken at a favorite restaurant on Route 9. My friend and decades-long walking partner served us turkey kale soup and leftover pumpkin pie. While Larry and her husband watched a Syracuse University football game, she helped me pick out age-appropriate toys for my five-month-old granddaughter. Another couple caught us up on people and upcoming events at the library, the book club, and the synagogue. I enjoyed our time with everyone greatly and realized again how much I missed having them in my life on a daily basis.

The most bittersweet moment for me during our time up north came when Larry and I visited our next door neighbors, a couple with whom we had shared pot lucks, perennials, and cups of sugar for thirty-six years. They caught us up with all that had happened on Devon Court since we had left. As I looked out their window and saw "our" house, it hit me that the pretty grey house with the blue shutters on the large wooded lot wasn't ours anymore. Our house and our lives were now in Florida.

In his poem, "Death of the Hired Man," Robert Frost said, "Home is the place where, when you have to go there, they have to take you in." Larry and I didn't **have** to go back to the Capital Region for Thanksgiving. We chose to go back. For us, the Capital District will be the place in our hearts where we have and will continue to have treasured memories. It is the place where family and friends will always take us in as if we had never left. And no matter how much I love Florida or any other place life will take me, I will always be coming home to Upstate New York.

FORTY TWO

What Makes Us the Same? Trip to Shoah Museum Inspires Writer to Find Commonality

On a recent visit to Portland, Oregon, Larry and I visited the Holocaust Memorial. A pathway strewn with bronze sculptures of unfinished lives—a violin, a teddy bear, a torn prayer book—brought us to a curved wall. Two columns were engraved with the brief history of the events that led to Hitler's rise and its unfathomable consequences on Europe and the world. Plaques etched with memories from survivors are placed on a wall representing barbed wire. One read "As I looked back, my mother turned her face to avoid mine and my little sister gave me a frail and knowing wave;" another, "The fear has never left me." On the back of wall were carved the names of family members of Oregonians who were lost in the Shoah. Below the names was the following statement:

Our precious life rests not on our ability to see what makes us different, one from another, but rather on our ability to recognize what makes us the same. What ultimately defines us is the moral strength to believe in our common humanity, and to act on this belief.

These words struck me especially hard on that beautiful June afternoon. Larry and I had flown out of Florida just days after the

Orlando Pulse tragedy. As I stood in front of the memorial, I was overwhelmed with grief for all those lost in the Shoah. I also thought of those innocent lives lost to another madman who could only focus on differences and destroy so many lives with another act of senseless violence. I began to reflect on my own live and question as to whether I had done enough to focus on "what makes us the same."

As a child, I knew I was different from most of the people in our small upstate New York town. Along with one other family, we were eleven Jews in a Christian town, an overwhelming .5% of the population. There were a few anti-Semitic instances: a teenage boy yelling "Heil Hitler!" and giving me the Nazi salute as the six-year-old me played innocently on my front yard; "lost" invitations to parties by those my parents tagged as anti-Semites; whispered jokes about my Jewish nose that went unnoticed by my teachers. For the most part, however, the people of Keeseville embraced us, shared their Christmas trimming with us; came over for matzoh brie around our Formica covered kitchen table. We focused on what we have in common.

Although exposed to diversity on our family's visits to New York City, as a student at University at Albany, and through—as always—countries and cultures explored through reading, my everyday encounters rarely took me far from my white, Judeo-Christian environment. This changed, however, when I took a teaching position with the Capital District Educational Opportunity Center

The EOC, a division of Hudson Valley Community College, offers tuition-free academic and workforce development opportunities to disadvantaged and educationally under-prepared New York State residents sixteen years and older. Through my interactions with staff and students, I learned to appreciate many different cultures and backgrounds and their personal struggles. A Muslim pharmacist, after being imprisoned in her native country for giving medicine to a Christian, disguised herself as a Bedouin to flee to Egypt then to Albany. A young man had escaped with his family as one of the Vietnamese boat people. Both completed our GED and College

Preparation Program and then graduated from Hudson Valley Community College. One of my fellow instructors had overcome a troubled background in Schenectady's inner city to graduate from the cosmetology program, open his own salon, and then come back to the EOC to instruct hundreds of cosmetology students in the technical and life skills needed to succeed in his chosen field.

I may have taught my students essay writing and grammar and study skills, but the people I encountered at the EOC taught me about courage and dignity and overcoming incredible obstacles. Our differences were secondary to our common goal of creating a better life for ourselves and our families. We all believed in our common humanity and acted on those beliefs. Even when I moved out of the classroom and into an administrative position, my greatest joy was meeting with students, having them share their personal histories with me, and my helping to promote the EOC through their many inspiring success stories.

In the weeks that followed, our country experienced more tragedies that resulted from actions by those who failed to believe in the common humanity: Orlando, Florida; St. Paul, Minnesota; Baton Rouge, Louisiana; Dallas, Texas. The list of cities where incidents of senseless violence continues to grow.

"There may be times when we are powerless to prevent injustice," wrote the late Elie Wiesel, "but there must never be a time when we fail to protest." My protests may not take me to the streets, but it will take me to the written word, where I hope I can make a difference.

But maybe, it must start with children. When we lived in Clifton Park, our next door neighbors were an interracial couple—he a Caucasian from Massachusetts and she a Whitney Houston look-alike from Jamaica. We shared our yards and our lives with them and their four children who have inherited their mother's brown eyes, mocha skin, and curly hair. One day, Julie and Katie, who were the same age, were shopping for matching lockets. When we brought the jewelry up to the counter, Julie, my blue eyed, blonde haired daughter, announced to the sales clerk, "I know we look like twin sisters. We're not. We're just best friends."

Best friends. Or just friends or neighbors or fellow citizens. Whatever it takes, let us all strive to recognize what makes us the same, to prevent injustice, to repair the world. *Tikkun Olam. Amen.*

ABOUT THE AUTHOR

MARILYN COHEN SHAPIRO grew up in a very close knit family in a small town on Lake Champlain in upstate New York. Since retiring from a career in adult education and relocating to Florida, she is now writing down family stories she has thought about during her entire life. She and her husband Larry are proud to have raised two children who enjoy reading, learning, and traveling as much as they do. Marilyn loves singing along to Broadway musicals, getting lost on well-marked trails in national parks, and eating vanilla ice cream.

Marilyn has been a regular contributor to the bi-weekly publication, *The Jewish World* (Schenectady NY), since 2013. *There Goes My Heart* is her first book. You may email her at *shapcomp18@gmail.com.*